Weaving

THE ART OF SUSTAINABLE TEXTILE CREATION

Weaving

THE ART OF SUSTAINABLE TEXTILE CREATION

SCHIFFER
PUBLISHING

4880 Lower Valley Road · Atglen, PA 19310

Maria Sigma

© 2020 design and layout BlueRed Press Ltd.
© 2020 text and imagery Maria Sigma

Photography Credits
Simon Clay Front cover and pages 3, 4/5, 12/13, 18/19, 62/63, 72, 81 bottom right, 82, 89, 90, 98/99, 112, 123, 124, 139, 140/141, 162, 167, 168, 175.
Alun Callender pages 6, 9, 15.

All other photography Maria Sigma

Library of Congress Control Number: 2020933417

Produced by BlueRed Press Ltd, 2020
Designed by Insight Design Concepts Ltd.
Type set in Gotham snd Neutra text

ISBN: 978-0-7643-6038-1
Printed in Hong Kong

Published by Schiffer Publishing, Ltd.
4880 Lower Valley Road
Atglen, PA 19310
Phone: (610) 593-1777; Fax: (610) 593-2002
Email: Info@schifferbooks.com
Web: www.schifferbooks.com

For our complete selection of fine books on this and related subjects, please visit our website at www.schifferbooks.com. You may also write for a free catalog.

Schiffer Publishing's titles are available at special discounts for bulk purchases for sales promotions or premiums. Special editions, including personalized covers, corporate imprints, and excerpts, can be created in large quantities for special needs. For more information, contact the publisher.

We are always looking for people to write books on new and related subjects. If you have an idea for a book, please contact us at proposals@schifferbooks.com.

Other Schiffer Books on Related Subjects:

Weave It!: 15 Fun Weaving Projects for Kids, Maria Sigma, ISBN 978-0-7643-6065-7

Artisan Felting: Wearable Art, Jenny Hill, ISBN 978-0-7643-5852-4

Artistry in Fiber, Vol. 1: Wall Art, Anne Lee, E. Ashley Rooney, Foreword by Marcia Young, Introduction by Meredith Re' Grimsley, ISBN 978-0-7643-5304-8

Contents

Introduction

For as long as I can remember, I have enjoyed making things. Being dyslexic, I found hands-on tasks a great alternative to anything that required language skills. Thanks to my mother, I was able to try a few arts and crafts, such as embroidery, ceramics, dance, music, painting, and drawing—I particularly enjoyed the latter. I loved color and relished the different textures the paint left when using a variety of brushes, pastels, or pencils. I also really enjoyed the messy feel and result of applying the pigments with my fingers!

I first came across textile making while spending summer school vacations with my grandparents on the Greek island of Andros in the Cyclades. My great-grandmother taught me how to crochet traditional Cycladic lace. I remember enjoying the repetitive nature of crocheting, the use of the hook, and especially the feeling of the yarn on my fingers, but I found the idea of just making white lace quite boring (how much lace could a kid use?). I also missed color.

The years passed and I completely forgot about crocheting until my first degree in textile conservation, where I came across a variety of different textile-making techniques, including crocheting. It reminded me and I started crocheting again, but this time with much chunkier and colorful yarns. However, it was only when I tried handweaving that I felt that all the pieces of the puzzle dropped into place—this craft combined creativity, math, design, texture, and the use of tools and machinery. It led me to take a second degree in textile design, specializing in handweaving.

Now, years later, I run my own small textile business in London, making handwoven zero-waste textiles for interiors. I also run workshops focusing on upcycling materials through weaving.

This book is an extension from my "Weaving from Waste" workshops, and it is designed to give you a thorough and intensive grounding in handweaving with a frame and with a heddle board, all with a focus on using waste materials. You will learn foundation weaving skills, such as warping, loom setup, color blending, and structure, as well as basic weaving techniques and patterns.

However, the aim of this book is not limited to just covering a wide range of styles through the guided projects, but also to inspire and give you a taste for improvisation and to encourage you to develop your own distinctive weaving voice and style.

Weaving: The Art of Sustainable Textile Creation introduces something new into old weaving techniques. The book uses illustrated instructions, step-by-step formats, and accessible language to show you a variety of things you can create with a basic weaving setup at home.

You don't need to be a crafter or have any previous experience in weaving to be able to take these projects on. With the help of the instructions and lots of practice, you will be able to complete even the most challenging projects. Accordingly, there is a basic practice section before each different type of weaving (frame weaving, circular weaving, band weaving), and each project is designed to teach you something new and "push" your weaving skills a bit further each time.

Try out the techniques. Test them, adapt them to your style, then make art pieces and objects that reflect your personality. Remember, there are no strict rules when it comes to crafting. All the instructions are only suggestions that I have found useful throughout my experience as a weaver and teacher— see this book as a guide to help you start weaving and learn something new. Here's wishing you the best of luck and joy in your weaving journey.

Philosophy and Sustainability

The core of my philosophy on textiles lies in producing high-quality interior products that are free of superfluous elements. However, at the same time I want to pay close attention to sustainability and usability. I want to emphasize the texture and materials in such a way that the products become timeless heirlooms and preserve their value through the years.

Zero Waste

My intention is to create aesthetically engaging and functional textiles by using the ideas and practices of zero-waste and sustainable design. Through a juxtaposition of modern-day and traditional craft techniques, my work is aimed at vivid but minimal textiles that creatively illustrate long-established techniques and styles to yield a vigorously current and environmentally sustainable product.

The craft of weaving is all around us, constantly present yet often unnoticed—it's used in everything from daily essentials to high-end designs. Fabrics not only occupy literally every corner of households everywhere around the world but are also a part of our body, being both a boundary and connection between people and nature. These things are interlinked into our culture and into memories themselves.

My sources of inspiration spring from these very human connections and the way we use textiles and make them an intrinsic part of our culture. My ideal view is a constant process of creating a product of high aesthetics through simplicity and the use of natural and sustainable materials, to end up with timeless objects.

I think of this as the philosophy of my work—values striving to reach a natural balance between an ethical sustainability of materials versus the pure aesthetics of a creation. In this book I try to inject these ideas of sustainability and a harmonic relationship between human-product and environment because we cannot just have either aesthetically pleasing objects or a healthy planet. We need both—zero waste.

I would like to express the whole concept of zero waste with a very simple but essential notion: we absolutely have to overcome the illusion that we live in a world with infinite resources—we most certainly don't. Now more than ever, everything depends on us and our actions for sustaining the quality of life and life itself on this beautiful blue planet.

My concept of textile design and making reflects my dedication to zero-waste design. I strive toward leaving minimum yarn waste, making no unnecessary cuts, treading the lightest feasible carbon footprint, and using as little as possible machinery, water, and electrical energy. By adhering to a zero-waste philosophy, I aspire to make handweaving an even more sustainable craft than ever before.

Is the textile industry really impacting the environment that much?

Yes, of all types of industry, the textile industry has a prominent position in impacting the environment in a negative way, due to a vicious circle of profit versus quality. Big manufacturers seeking larger profits are producing unnecessarily huge quantities of products with fast turnarounds—in particular, so-called "fast fashion."

Unfortunately, this means that the quality of these products tends to be poor because of the speed of their creation. And because of this poor quality, they fall apart and are thrown away more quickly.

The two most devastating results of these tactics are a horrific waste of water and land for such production, and an ever-growing amount of waste products due to their lower quality. It's easier for customers to replace them by buying again and again, and it's become what many people expect.

We need to reduce not only the volume but also the toxicity of the materials we use. We need sustainable and reusable products that don't need to be burned or buried when they are no longer wanted, to allow a pace of natural regeneration in the world we live in.

Are things really changing?

Zero-waste philosophy is not a new idea. It has been with us for centuries as people reused and re-created textiles and clothes for reasons of ethical choice or necessity. This necessity comes hand in hand with aesthetics. Many of use will remember a grandmother or friend who repurposed an old shirt to make another useful garment.

Over the last few years there has been a growing number of eco-conscious consumers, new ethical makers, and up-and-coming designers who challenge the old fast-fashion business model and insist on a sensible approach to production. The benefits of a zero-waste approach, and reuse-recycle ethos, are not only environmental, but they positively affect our societal ethics, our view of the world, and the larger global economy itself.

Most importantly, an economy that relies on zero waste and a circular model of reusing materials has the chance of creating many more jobs to deal with the recycling of materials. In the long run this will create the conditions for a better quality of life, while simultaneously prolonging the endurance of valuable resources for many more generations to come.

Professionally, I have always been aware that I could not avoid linking the production of my textiles with their environmental footprint. I strive for new solutions that could change the way consumers think about textile waste, and I include these practices in my craft.

Regardless of the size of my projects—even those in this book—my underlying goal is an efficient, ethical, and economical one. It is a simple model where all discarded materials become resources for newer projects, thus minimizing any waste, while also keeping the work economic. The beauty of this practice leads to the balance of merging used or pure undyed materials into an aesthetically pleasing world of their own—it's a way of mimicking nature that is self-sufficient in its cycles.

A zero-waste philosophy for our designs is much more than just recycling. Recycling, although being one-third of the triptych "Reduce, Reuse, Recycle," is only a part of what we can achieve.

Reducing as consumers and reusing as creators and craft-minded people is a one-way street and the only viable vision for the future. Such a practice—apart from its obvious benefits on the environment, to our societies, and to our economy—plays a huge role as a paradigm for the future of our society and eventually in ourselves and of our very conscience.

Creating with a zero-waste design philosophy is truly a liberating process that leads to a better self.

Feeling at Home
Textiles play a great role in making us feel "at home." It only takes a glance at our surroundings to realize how many of the most mundane things around us are made out of fabric: obviously our clothes, which like a second skin mediate between our body and nature, but almost everywhere else on floors, tables, beds, and windows. Where we eat, where we sleep, and where we sit, textiles provide a sense of the familiar and the beloved.

Textiles show our community who we are or separate us from it. They give each individual an identity (the power of fashion), enriching this personal identity, or provide a collective one (uniforms of all kinds). In any case, they always indicate our position in society—it's the most private and simultaneously the most public signal. Flags, turbans, saris, Islamic hijab, hats, or men's ties—the list is endless: they all allude to whole worlds of semiotics, indicating ideology and desires, actual or not. The real and the symbolic have always been tied to the preparation and the creation of textiles.

The symbolic side of textiles is linked historically with issues of enormous importance to people and society. Take the great metaphor of life and death found in the Greek mythology where the three Fates spin destiny, measure its length, and cut the thread of life. It was believed that the thread of life was spanned twice during one's lifetime, first at birth and second at marriage, since these are the two most important events in a person's life.

Passed on from one generation to another, textile heirlooms become narrative objects of great sentimental value, which encompass a particular sense of belonging—of feeling at home.

Why Craft (Weaving) Matters
Living in a digital era of single-use objects, where people discard things easily, the need for tangible and real materials arises. Craft is more than just a way of making things: for me

it's a way of thinking and living in the most sustainable and meaningful way.

Craft questions the different processes of dealing with the material world, and it brings back a certain level of human dignity. Craft calms down our high-speed society, and in a way it's a tool to connect our past with our present. Craft can invest a context of regionalism and history to our convenience-based economy. Craft is an event that starts with a physical sense of relationship between materials and people. More specifically, handweaving—one of the oldest crafts—is like a portal to past eras and candlelit work environments; it brings back a long-forgotten collaboration of the body and the mind, and the relationship between domesticity and creativity.

Handcrafted goods remind us how and why we are human—they carry a story, the maker's personality, and the emotional state of their creator. On handwoven textiles you can often see signs of where the weaver has taken a break from the loom; something that otherwise is an industrial defect becomes a detail we can empathize with.

That is why we need more weavers and crafters in the world. With this book I hope that you will start your weaving journey and you will feel confident enough to carry on discovering your own path and weaving style.

What Is Weaving?

What Is Weaving?

Weaving is a method of textile production in which two distinct sets of yarns or threads are interlaced at right angles to form a fabric or cloth.

The longitudinal threads are called the warp, and the lateral threads are the weft. (Weft is an old English word meaning "that which is woven.") The method in which these threads are interwoven affects the characteristics of the cloth.

Cloth is usually woven on a loom, a wooden construction or machinery that holds the warp threads in place while the weft is woven through them. A fabric band that meets this definition of cloth (warp threads with a weft thread winding between) can also be made using alternative methods, including tablet weaving, backstrap, or other techniques without looms.

The way the warp and filling threads interlace with each other is called the weave. The majority of woven products are created with one of three basic weaves: plain weave, satin weave, or twill. Woven cloth can be plain (in one color or a simple pattern) or can be woven in a decorative, simple, or complicated artistic design.

Plain Weave

Also known as tabby weave, linen weave, or taffeta weave, this is the most basic weaving pattern. It is strong and hard wearing and is used for fashion and furnishing fabrics. In plain-weave cloth, the warp and weft threads cross at right angles, aligned so they form a simple crisscross pattern. Each weft thread crosses the warp threads by going over one, then under the next, and so on. The next weft thread goes under the warp threads that the previous one went over, and vice versa. Plain weave is the oldest and commonest weave in the world.

Satin Weave

Characterized by four or more weft yarns floating over a warp yarn, satin weave is associated with luxury, romance, and sensuousness and has the best draping qualities of all the weave types. Satin weave is one of three basic weave structures that have been in use since ancient times. It has a smooth, lustrous surface and a dull back side, with predominant weft yarns on the face of the cloth.

Twill

This is one of the three fundamental textile weaves (with plain and satin weave), with a characteristic pattern of diagonal parallel ribs. It is made by passing the weft yarn over one (or more) warp threads, then under two (or more) warp threads and so on, with an offset between rows to create the characteristic diagonal pattern. Twill is popular because it is very durable and hides stains well. It is used for denim jeans, chinos, furniture coverings, bags, and much more.

Terminology

Beater
A weighted tool with "teeth" used to beat down the weft once it has passed through the warp. This can be a specialist weaving/tapestry comb or beater, or simply ordinary combs or just ordinary metal or wooden forks.

Cloth
The finished textile—a flexible material consisting of a network of natural or artificial fibers (yarn or thread)

Rotating heddle bar
Used to separate the warp and make it easier for the weft to pass through; each warp thread is passed through one heddle. A heddle can be (1) a rotating stick that has grooves for the warp threads, (2) wires and strings that pull on the warp threads to separate them, or (3) a rigid heddle, which is a single piece with slots that either pull the warp threads up or down to create the shed (*see below*). Rotating heddle bars are used to separate the warp, helping speed up the weaving process by creating an opening—the weaving shed—between alternating warp threads.

Loom
The structure that holds your weave, it supports and controls the tension as you work. Once your weave is complete, you will cut it off the loom, and your weave will have its own structure. Looms can vary enormously in shape and size, from the extremely large floor looms down to small handheld looms. There are also circular looms that allow the user to weave in a circle.

Picks
Every weft row interlaced into the woven cloth is called a pick. In the textile industry the density of a woven cloth is measured in picks per inch.

Shed
This is the gap that separates the warp threads that create upper and lower warp sets that you pass the weft thread through. Creating a shed between your warp threads speeds up your weaving. When using a frame loom, a shed stick can be threaded between the warp threads, then turned on its side to create the shed between the warps. Some frame looms come with a rotating heddle to create the shed.

Shuttle
A tool designed to neatly and compactly store a holder that carries the thread of the weft yarn while weaving. Shuttles are thrown or passed back and forth through the shed between the warp, in order to weave in the weft. The simplest shuttles, known as "stick shuttles," are made from a flat, narrow piece of wood with notches on the ends to hold the weft yarn. More complicated shuttles (known as boat shuttles) incorporate bobbins or pins.

Tapestry needle
Can be used to weave different shapes and colors into your piece, particularly in small areas, or when your yarn is too chunky to go around the shuttle. A tapestry needle can also be used to weave in loose yarn at the back.

Warp
The thread (or group of threads) that is strung over the loom vertically and holds the tension while you weave. This is the backbone of your weave.

Weft
The thread that you weave (pass) horizontally between, around, and over the warp threads. It creates your patterns and design in the weave.

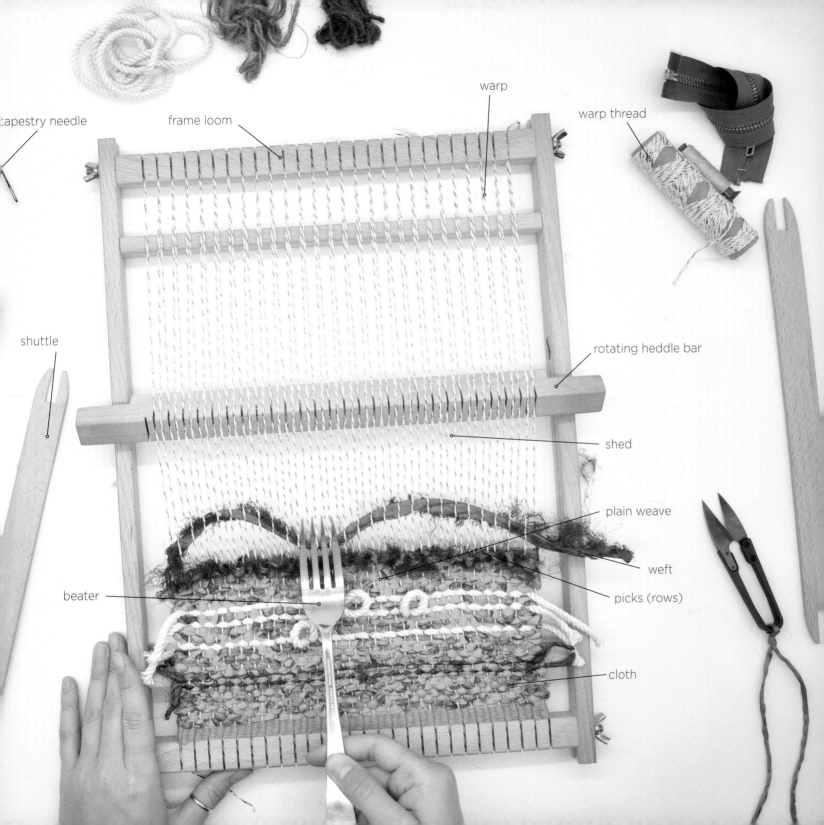

tapestry needle

frame loom

warp

warp thread

shuttle

rotating heddle bar

shed

plain weave

weft

beater

picks (rows)

cloth

Frame Weaving

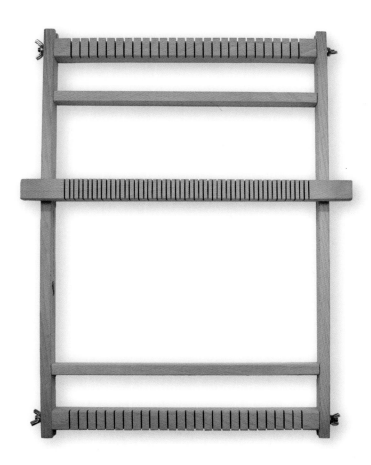

Frame Weaving

Frame weaving uses a frame set up as a loom. It is also called lap weaving. Frame weaving is closer to tapestry weaving, since the warp is mainly invisible and covered by the weft. However, that also depends on the thickness of the weft.

On a frame loom (depending on its size) you can weave a variety of beautiful things. You can make an art piece for the wall or make useful pieces such as rugs, table mats, clutch bags, bookmarks, and pieces for garment decoration.

Frame weaving is the best first step to start your weaving journey. Weaving can seem a bit complicated because it requires a lot of steps: it is not. You just need to follow the steps and practice until you get familiar with the equipment, tools, and materials. After you understand the process, it's pretty easy and can be very meditative as well.

For all following steps, I am using a loom with a rotating heddle bar and adjustable top and bottom beams. These help you speed up the weaving process by creating an opening (known as a weaving shed) between alternating warp threads. In addition, the rotating heddle bar also allows you to control the tension even after you have warped the loom—by rotating the beams toward the outside or inside.

The bar has two rotating positions—toward the top beam or toward the bottom beam. In each position it separates the warp by lifting the odd/even warp threads. By alternatively rotating the bar between the two positions, you are able to weave tabby (plain weave).

Note: With a different warping and process of taking off the loom, all other steps can also apply on any frame loom.

Designing Your Piece (or Not)

Before you start weaving, it is good to have an idea of what you want to make. This can be a very detailed idea, already predesigned on paper as a sketch or drawing. Alternatively, you can just have something in mind or an inspirational image to work toward.

You could, of course, have no idea and instead improvise while weaving based on the materials you have and your mood. It is up to you! It really depends on your personality and why you are weaving—whether it's for relaxation and fun, to improve your creativity and artistic voice, or to make useful things—or all of the above!

It is important to remember that there are no rights and wrongs. All the steps in this book are suggestions about how to weave on a frame loom that I have been taught or discovered throughout my weaving experience. Of course, I have made many mistakes during my weaving journey—some were awful and some ended up being happy accidents—but only through mistakes can you learn something new.

From the moment you decide to start your weaving journey, you need to remind yourself that you are now the weaver, you are the designer, you are the boss. You make decisions based on your taste and personality. Anything you make is perfect as long as you like it. Feel free to make your own mistakes and to discover different ways to do things that suit you better, as well as ways that make more sense to you.

Choosing a Warp Thread
Warp Thread Characteristics
When designing any woven piece, your choice of warp thread should be carefully considered, since it will form the foundation of your fabric and be the structure on which you weave. It should be strong and smooth and be able to withstand the friction and stretching created by the weaving process.

Warp thread is usually made of cotton or linen and consists of a number of threads, hard twisted for strength and durability. The natural smoothness of cotton or linen ensures that your weaving yarn will pass smoothly across the warp.

Finding a Substitute
If you don't have an obvious tapestry warp at hand, I recommend finding another strong three- or four-ply cotton/linen thread such as crochet cotton, gardening string, cotton wrapping twine, etc. You can also experiment with other yarns and materials (hemp, acrylic, wool, etc.). Try to avoid unusual (often expensive) yarns that have very little twist, since they will be more likely to snap.

Warp Suggestions
- baker's (cotton) twine (**a**)
- butcher's (rayon) twine (**b**)
- recycled cotton string—3 ply, 1.5 mm (**c**)
- crochet (cotton/bamboo) yarn, lace weight (**d**)
- cotton string—4 ply, 1 mm (**e**)
- linen string—4 ply, 1 mm (**f**)

Check and tighten the four screws on the sides of your frame. Make sure that both top and bottom beams are tightly in place and lying flat, with the "teeth" facing outward.

1. Take the end of your warp thread and tie a double knot on the first gap at the top right of your frame.

2. Stretch your thread and insert it in the first gap on the right side of the bottom beam.

3. Loop the thread around the tooth to the left of your warping area and go back to the first gap on the top beam.

Note: The warp should have an even tension across the loom and feel springy when plucked.

To avoid uneven tension, keep checking the tension as you warp, and tighten any loose threads as you go—don't wait until you finish the threading.

Warping

You will need:
Frame loom with a rotating
  heddle bar
Scissors
82 ft. (25 m) cotton/linen for
  the warp

1a

2

1b

3a

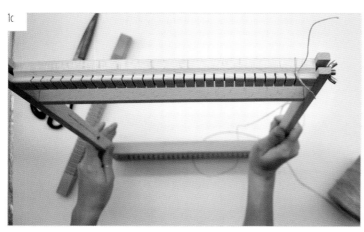

1c

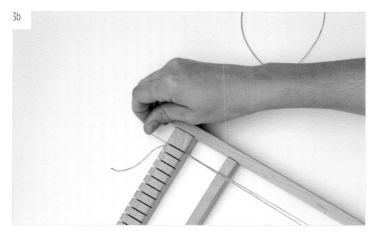

3b

4. While keeping the tension, loop the thread around the tooth on the left-hand side of your warping area and go back to the second gap on the bottom beam.

5. Carry on repeating steps 3 and 4, by working across to the left side. Keep checking your tension as you go.

6. To finish the warping, carry the thread until you get to the last gap on the bottom beam. Then go all around the bottom beam with your tail and then around and under the last warp thread twice. Make sure to keep the tension tight. Cut the warp thread, leaving a tail of about 4 inches. Secure it with a double knot between the tail and the last warp thread.

7. Now it's time to insert the rotating heddle bar. Turn your loom over and place the diagonal bar inside the loom, with the teeth of the bar facing toward the warp threads. Then, with your thumbs, push the bar so it is placed over the loom frame in the front.

Turn your loom over again and move the bar so it is horizontal to the frame loom.

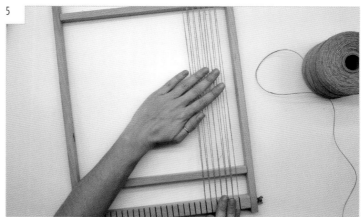

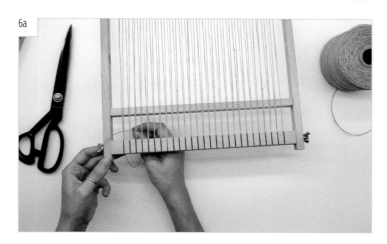

6b

7a

6c
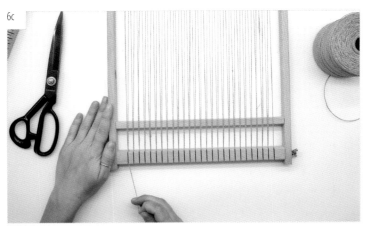

7b

6d

7c
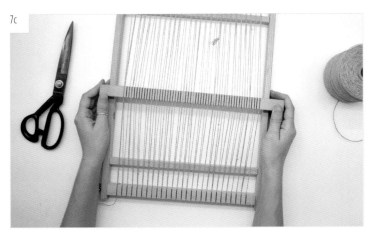

8. Last, but not least, you need to make sure that all the warp threads are sitting in the bar's gaps, one by one and in the right order—with no twisting or overlapping.

9. Now check your tension. If it feels loose, you can adjust it and make it a bit tighter by rotating the bottom or the top beam (or both) slightly toward the outside.

You are now ready to weave!

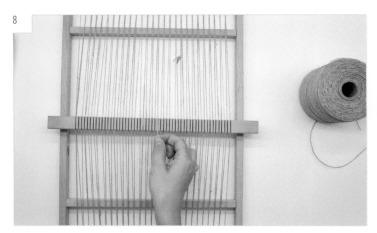

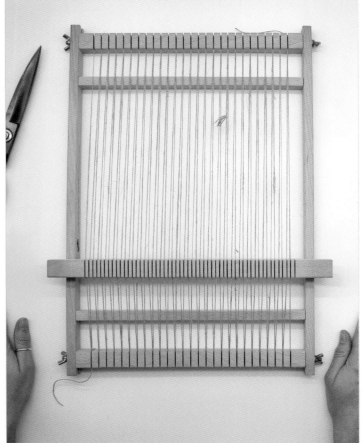

Beginning to Weave

On a frame loom, start weaving from the bottom and work up to the top. It is helpful to think that you are "building" your piece—like building a wall with bricks—so every weft pick is a row of bricks.

When you are making shapes, it is important not to leave gaps, since it is difficult to go back and weave them in (fill them)—just as it would be difficult to go back and fill an empty space on the wall with bricks. It is much better to try to build your piece evenly along the width.

You can, of course, leave an empty space if a negative space is part of your design.

Plain Weave

You will need:
Your warped loom
3 colored weft yarns
Fork
Scissors
2 shuttles
Snip scissors
Tapestry needle
Warp thread

To give rigidity to your weaving, the first few rows (and the last few rows) of your piece should be woven with a thin yarn similar to your warp's thickness. Weavers usually use their warp threads as the weft for these rows, but you could instead choose another yarn if the warp color does not suit your piece's color palette, or you want a contrast color. I usually use the warp thread; it adds the impression of a frame to the piece as a whole.

1. Wind a few rounds—about 6-8 turns—of your warp thread on the shuttle.

2. Rotate the heddle so that half of the warp is lifted (toward the top).

3. Before you start weaving, make sure you have extra yarn that's more than the width of your loom. Pass the shuttle all the way across, from right to left, through the shed (in between the warp).

Note: It does not matter which side you start your weaving.

4. Gently pull your excess yarn so that you end up with a tail of about 2 inches on the side you started. You will weave this tail in later on.

1a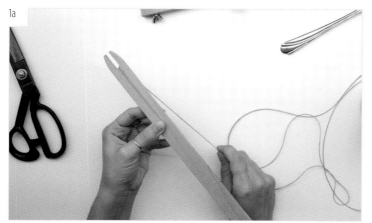

3a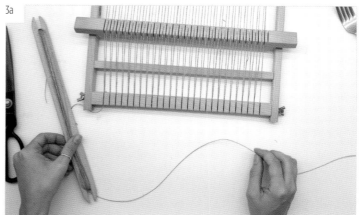

1b

3b

2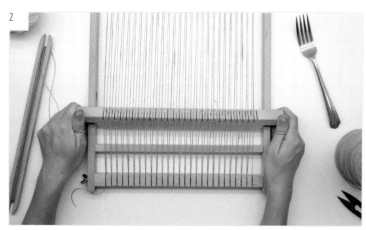

4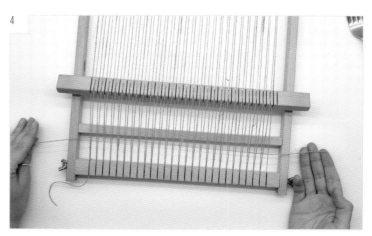

5. Pull the yarn down on either side to create a curve of about an inch high.

Note: You need more yarn than one straight line, because the yarn needs to go over and under the warp threads. By creating a curve you are adding extra length to your yarn.

6. Using your fork, beat down the weft, starting in the middle and then working from side to side.

7. Rotate the bar toward you.

8. First make sure you have enough loose weft—more than the width of your loom—and then pass your shuttle through the shed from the left side to the right side.

9. Pull any excess yarn and create another curve, but this time make sure that you don't pull too tight and squeeze the warp threads on the left. However, you must also be careful that you don't leave any loose yarn.

10. Press down the weft again—starting in the middle and then working out to the sides.

Note: By pressing the middle down first, you help the yarn spread evenly across the width.

7

9

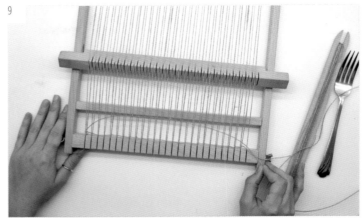

8a

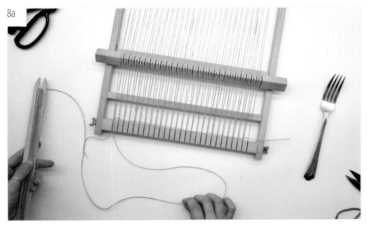

10

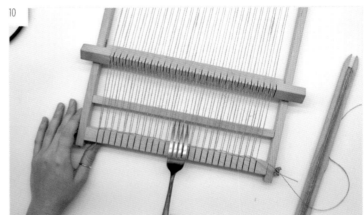

8b

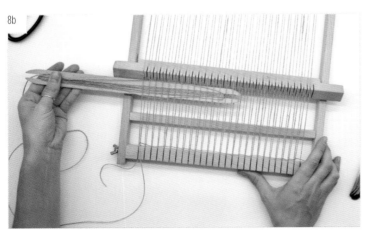

11. Before you move on to your next pick, you need to secure the tail of your first pick. The easiest and neatest way to do this is to weave it in with your fingers along with the second pick. Then just put it through the shed, tamp it down, and leave it to hang loose at the back.

12. Repeat the steps above until you have woven about a quarter of an inch—around ten picks.

13. When you have woven enough, cut your yarn and leave a tail of about 2 inches. Then change the position of the bar and weave the tail in with your fingers, as before.

And done! You can now start weaving your piece.

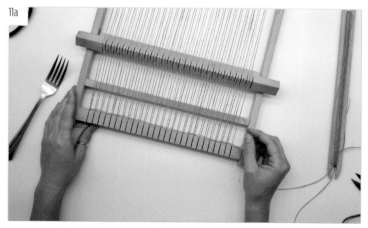

back side
of loom

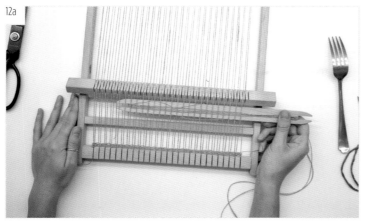

12a

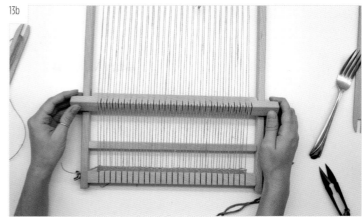

13b

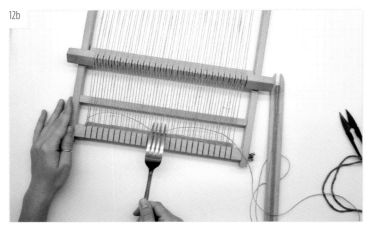

12b

13c

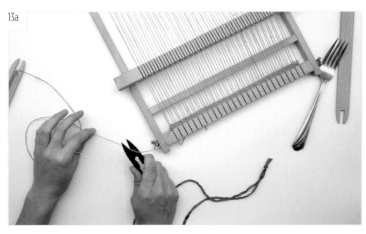

13a

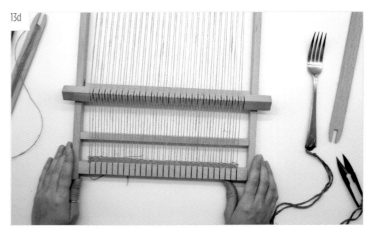

13d

Making a Fringe/Tassels

These are usually at the bottom of the piece, so in most cases they are added after the first plain-weave rows made with the warp thread.

They can also be added at the end of your piece—the technique is exactly the same. So, again, it's your choice. In the book I've demonstrated both ways, so you can decide which you prefer—it will depend on the piece.

Add a fringe at the beginning (bottom of the weave)

If your fringe is a key thing on your piece, I advise you to make it right at the start. Then, based on the color palette of the fringe and the sequence and proportions of the colors, you can build the rest of your piece. It is important to remember that in order for your piece to have a color consistency and balance, it is best to use all the yarns you have used in your fringe in the main weave itself.

Add a fringe at the end (top of your weave)

If you are not sure what you are making and you're going to improvise as you go, then I would advise you to add the fringe at the end of your piece, again based on the colors and yarns you have used. The advantage of adding fringing at the end is that you will get a cleaner and neater bottom, and you can hide the unused warp ends underneath the fringe (you can see what I am talking about on pp. 96–97).

How to add a fringe/tassels on your piece (bottom of your weave)

1. To make a fringe on your weave, first you need to decide what yarns and colors you want to have and how long and how thick you want the fringe to be.

2. Cut pieces of yarn—as many as you need for your desired thickness, but double the desired length.

3. With your bar on flat position, take a piece of yarn (or pieces of yarn) and pull it/them under both the first and second strings, so that the yarn hangs at an equal length down both sides.

1
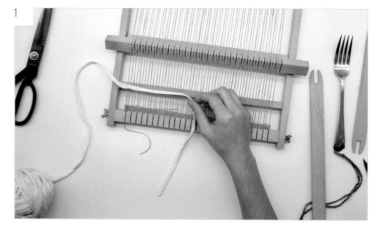

2a

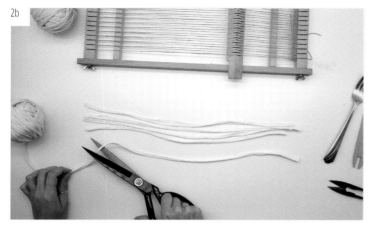

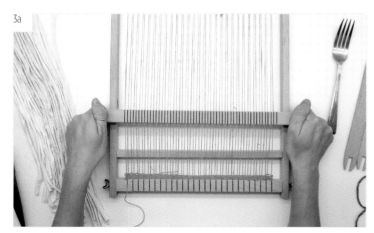

4. Make a loop by pulling through the middle of the yarn with your finger. Then, take both hanging lengths and pull them through the loop, keeping the length of the sides even. Individually pull each piece of yarn to make the knot tight and neat. This will give you a nice even fringe that sits flush on the previous row.

5. Repeat this process until you reach the other side. You will end up having a single warp thread remaining.

6. In order to add a tassel on the last single warp thread, take your length of yarn and pull the middle of it under the warp. Then, pull through the loop up and over the warp thread at the edge (like putting a scarf around your neck). Last, pull the edges to make the row tight and neat. Trim the tassel ends evenly with sharp scissors if you want a smart finish.

That's it!

Note: You can add a fringe or tassels at any point. The technique is the same. Even if you decide after you have finished your piece that a bit of fringe is just what's needed, you can usually make a bit of space and squeeze it in.

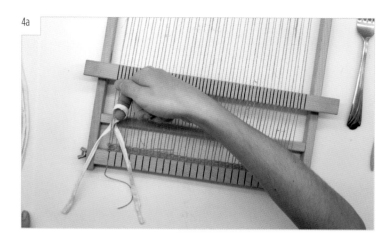

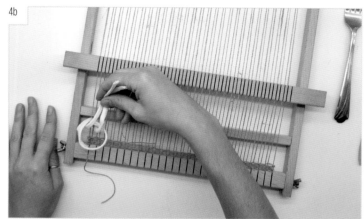

5a

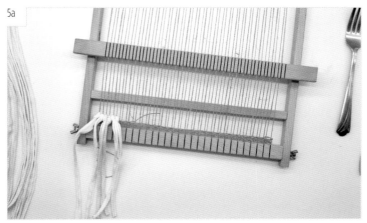

6a

5b

6b

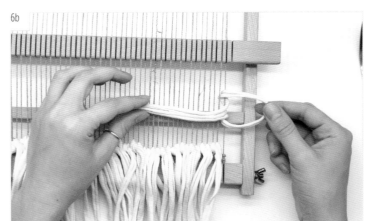

5c

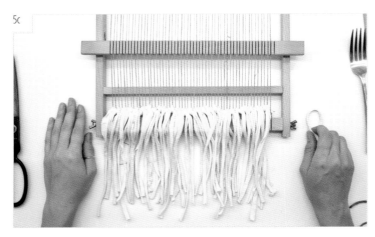

6c

Color Blending

Adding a feeling of depth to any woven piece, color-blending techniques have been used by weavers for centuries to create a new bespoke shade by using a blend of two colors.

One easy way to do this blending is to mix different wefts on the shuttle. This creates a marl effect on the loom. You can experiment with different shades of the same color, with contrasting textures, or with colors that are bold and clashing (see "Free Weaving" on pp. 50–52).

Another way to blend colors on the loom is to gradually introduce and increase the amount (number of rows) of one color while gradually decreasing the amount (rows) of the other color. Depending on the thicknesses of the yarns, you will end up with a gradual color change and a new shade in between if your yarns are thin, and with a stripy new color if your yarns are thick.

This is an example of a gradual color blending. It is best achieved by using two colored yarns of the same thickness—yarns A and B.

1. Wind a bit of yarn A onto your shuttle and weave five rows.

Note: Do not overload your shuttle, because it will not go through the shed; and remember to weave in your loose end (tail) at the beginning.

2. Wind a bit of yarn B onto your second shuttle. Without cutting yarn A, weave in just one row with color B, leaving an end. It's important that you do not weave in your loose end—because your next row will be with color A, and it will show. Remember to beat down your weft as your design progresses.

3. Weave four rows with yarn A. It's important that you ensure your yarn A will go over yarn B on the side that they meet.

1a

2a

1b

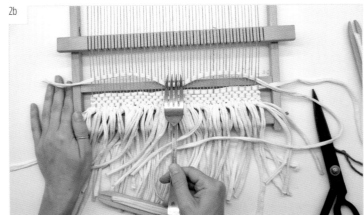

2b

1c

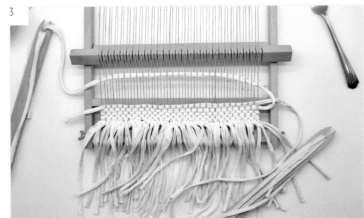

3

4. Weave two rows with yarn B (without cutting yarn A). You can now weave in your loose end too.

5. Weave three rows with yarn A.

> **What to do if you run out of yarn and you want to carry on with the same yarn**
> Since I dislike having knots on my pieces and am always trying to minimize waste, when I'm running out of yarn I just pretend that it doesn't matter! This means that I weave as much as I can with the yarn I have on my shuttle, and then I introduce more yarn and create a short overlap of about an inch where the yarns meet, and just leave a bit of loose end hanging out the back.

6. Weave three rows with yarn B.

7. Weave two rows with yarn A.

8. Weave four rows of yarn B.

9. Weave a row of yarn A, cut it off, and weave in the loose end.

10. Weave five rows of yarn B and cut it off. Weave in your loose end.

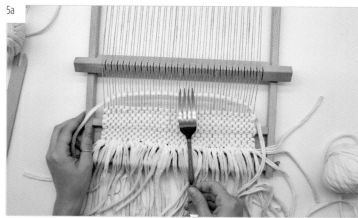

5c

8

6

9

7

10

Braid Weaving—Soumak Stitch

Soumak is a traditional tapestry technique for weaving strong and decorative textiles. The method involves wrapping the weft around the warp threads to add an embroidery-like pattern. Soumak stitch sits on top of the warp threads and adds some texture and dimension to the weave. Also, when two rows of soumak weave are put on top of each other, it creates a braid effect in your weave.

To make things clear, I have numbered the warps (starting from the right-hand side), but you can put a soumak stitch wherever you want in your weave.

1. Cut a long piece of yarn—about eight times the width of your loom—and put your heddle bar at the flat position.

2. Take the end of your yarn and make a knot around the first warp (#1) at the right-hand side of your loom. Weave the loose end in with your fingers as usual.

3. Loop the yarn around and behind warps #1 and #2 and pull through.

4. Loop the yarn over warp #1 and #2 and then under warps #1, #2, #3, and #4 and pull through.

5. Loop your yarn over warps #3 and #4 and go under warps #5 and #6, coming out at #6.

2b

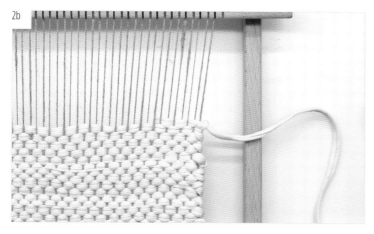

4

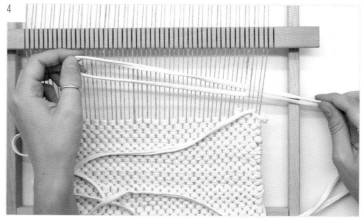

3a

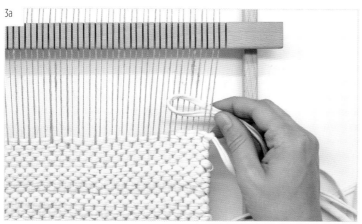

5

3b

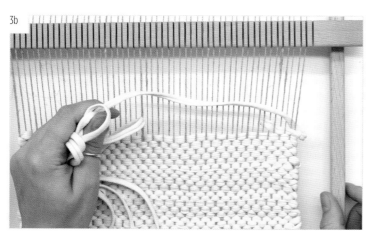

6. Repeat the last step until you reach the other side (or for as long as you wish). At the end, loop the yarn around just a single warp thread (since your total warp threads are an even number).

Note: Kept fairly loose, this stitch will give your braid more texture and make it look bolder.

7. In order to achieve the braid effect, you need to do one more row of soumak, but looping in the opposite direction. Take your yarn and loop it around and behind warps #2 and #3 (counting from the left side).

8. Carry on looping around and behind every two warp threads by working across toward the right side.

9. If you have enough yarn left, you can weave it on top of the soumak rows, beat down. If you have only a bit left, just weave it for about an inch to secure it, then carry on with your piece.

10. Last, gently pull the loops of the soumak rows to make them even and fluffy.

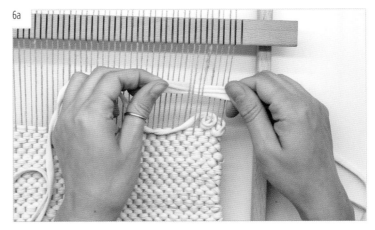

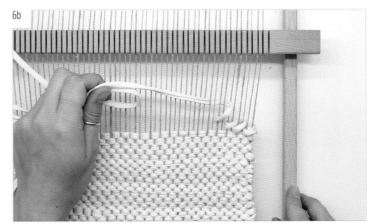

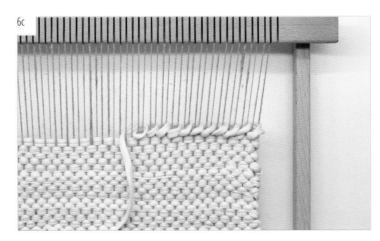

6d
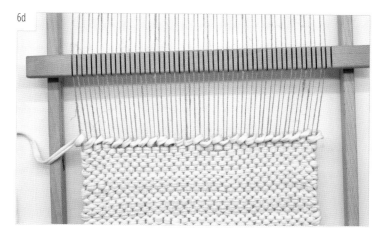

9a
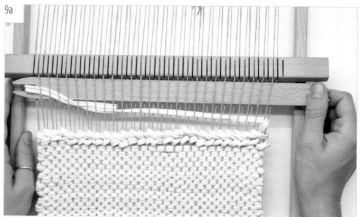

7

9b

8
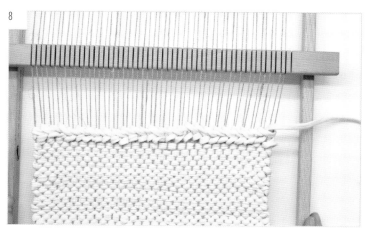

10
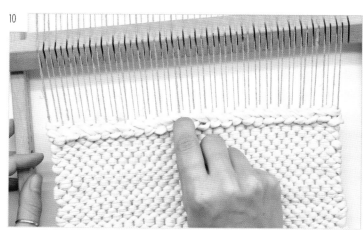

Color Blocks and Shapes

Wrongly thought to be tricky, color blocks and shapes are really quite easy to do. However, you need to be quite familiar with plain weave across the full width of your loom first. Weaving shapes is more like weaving in smaller areas than the full width of your loom. The tricky bit is that you need to work in multiple areas at the same time, since you cannot go back if you leave a gap.

Blocks

To weave a square or rectangular block is easy. You weave exactly as if doing the full width of the loom, but across a smaller area. You just weave the block area with the one color, then weave on the side (or sides) with another color.

Triangles/Diamonds

To weave a triangle or a diamond, you need to weave as normal on a smaller area and gradually increase or decrease the number of warps you are weaving. It is important to increase or decrease the same number of warp threads equally on both sides at the same time.

Circles

The most difficult shapes are circles, because when the weft meets the warp it creates small squares (think of them like pixels on an image). So, in order to make a circle out of small squares, you need to have the right size of squares. The size of the square depends on the thickness of the weft and the spacing between the warp threads. In order to achieve a neat circle, I advise you to experiment with different yarn thicknesses until you have the one that makes your circle nice and round.

Creating a triangle

You will need two colored yarns of similar thickness. Since I am making a triangle on the left edge with its apex pointing to the right, I start by weaving the background of the triangle. I leave unwoven space for the triangle to be woven in later on, because if I start with the triangle it will be very tricky to weave underneath it.

1. Start weaving with one of the colored yarns. Weave two rows (one full line) along all warp threads.

2. After each full line, skip one warp thread. Remember to regularly beat down your weft.

Tip: The number of rows are woven in between every skip, and the thickness of the yarn determines the angle of the triangle.

3. Carry on until you have unwoven space at the left, for half the triangle.

4. With your other color of yarn, start weaving the triangle. You can do this with your fingers or with a tapestry needle.

1

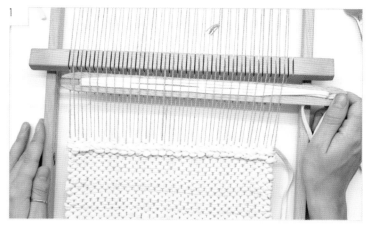

3

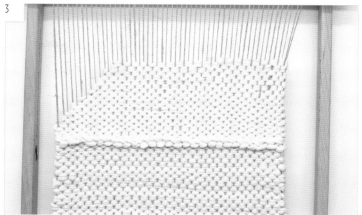

2a

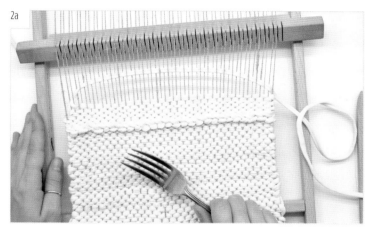

4a

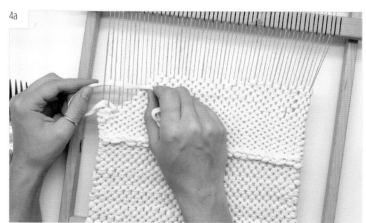

2b

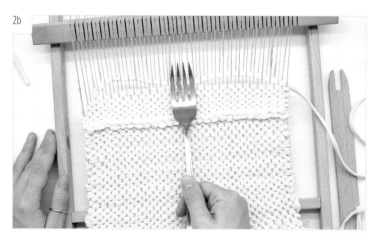

4b

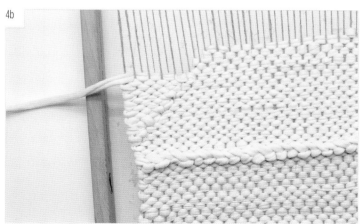

5. When you have woven up to the same level as the background color, you carry on weaving and start skipping one warp thread (on the left side) every two rows until you have only one warp thread to weave.

6. Return to your background color and weave the rest until you have filled up the side of the triangle.

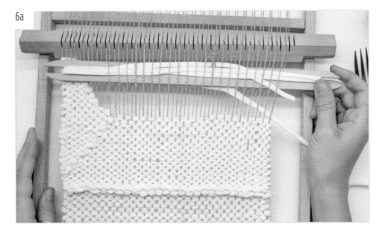

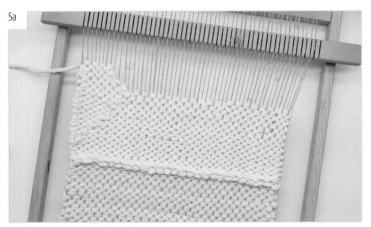

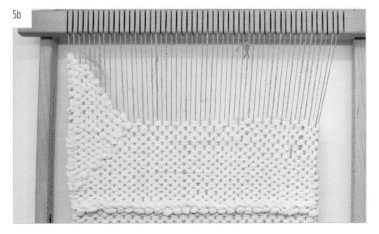

Note: Depending on the thickness of the yarns, there might be small gaps in the areas where the two yarns meet. They will close up after you've cut your piece off the loom, because the loom is stretching the weaving. However, if there are still visible gaps that bother you, they can be sewn up at the back.

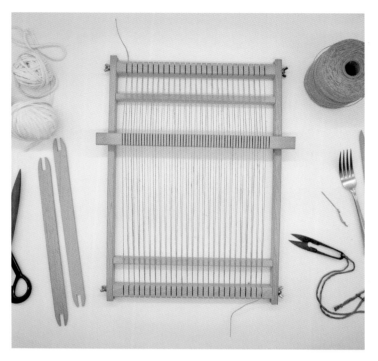

This is an example of free weaving and color blending by mixing up the wefts. To get the right effect, you'll need two or three colored yarns.

1. Take two pieces of yarn together and, with your tapestry needle (or fingers), start weaving a small area on your loom to create a curve. Increase the curve by one warp thread on either side of every row.

Note: If you are starting a new piece, don't forget to first weave the first few plain rows with your warp thread.

2. Carry on by weaving more areas in the same way.

Note: You can use the heddle bar as usual, or you can put it in the flat position and just go over and under the warp threads and vice versa on every row. In some areas you can even go over two and under two, and vice versa on the next row. Free weaving is perfect for experimentation and is what this type of crafting is all about.

Free Weaving

Free weaving means weaving with irregular wefts and is another way to build shapes on the loom. Instead of working vertically side to side, you manipulate your weft by creating flowing and undulating lines. The weft is not pressed evenly and flat but instead curves over and around woven areas. It is as if you are treating the warp as a net on which you freely create shapes, instead of building them like a wall with bricks.

Free weaving is great when you haven't planned your piece in advance and you just let your mood and materials guide you—it's called free for a reason! It can be mixed up with regular weaving, which will give it a rigidity and "secure" the shapes in place. It works best when using a not-too-slippery weft, such as wool, cotton, and natural fibers in general, so that the weaving stays in place and holds its shape.

1a

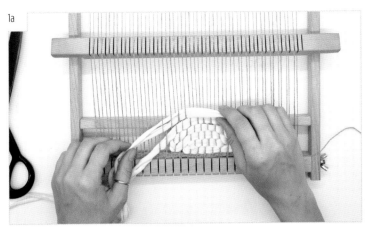

2a

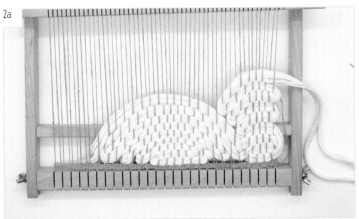

1b

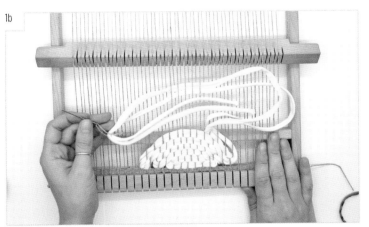

2b

1c

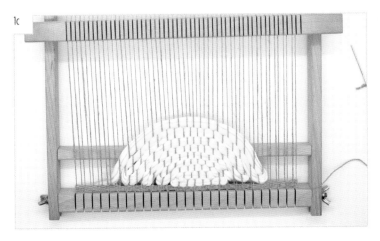

3. Add some regular weave into the empty areas and beat the weft down irregularly to create wavy shapes.

Carry on free weaving and creating curves. Play around with your colors by interlacing them into each other.

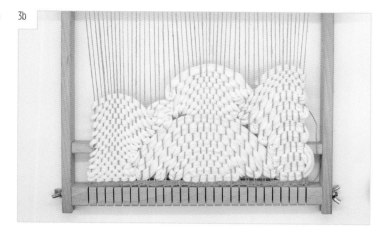

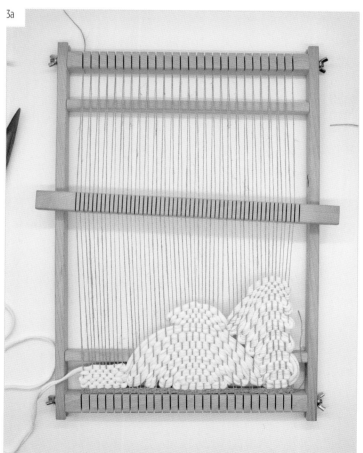

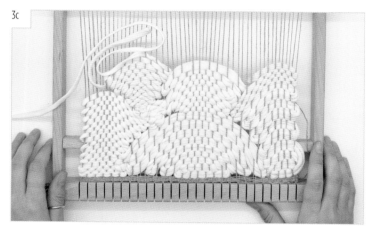

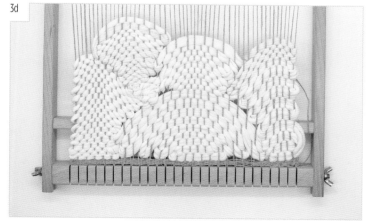

Braid Weaving—Rya Knot

You will need a long piece of yarn about eight times the width of your loom.

1. Take the middle of your yarn with one hand and, with your other fingers, pull the folded end under the first warp on the left side.

Tip: If you're using a thin yarn, I suggest that you thread it on a tapestry needle.

2. Bring the ends of the yarn through the loop and over the warp thread. Pull the knot tight.

3. Pass the ends of the yarn around the next two warp threads, from the front to the back (over and around). The ends will come out on the left-hand side of the loom. Pull the knot tight.

4. Carry on for as long as you wish.

Tip: If you have enough yarn ends left, you can weave them in. Otherwise, if they are too short, just leave them hanging loose at the back.

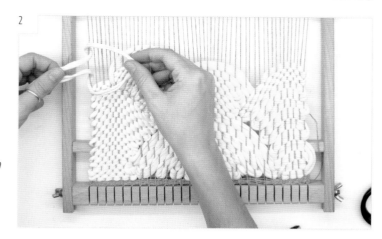

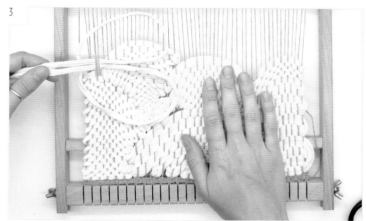

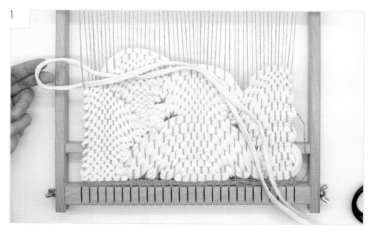

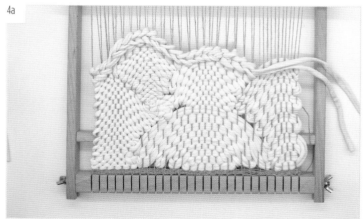

To add more texture to your piece, you can start from the other side and repeat the braiding on top.

Tip: *If your ends are long enough, you can incorporate them later on into your weaving.*

5. Important: When you've finished with your piece, don't forget to make a few plain-weave rows with your warp thread (for about half an inch) as you did at the beginning, to add some rigidity and to secure your weft.

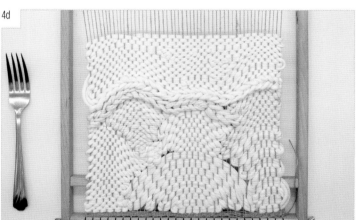

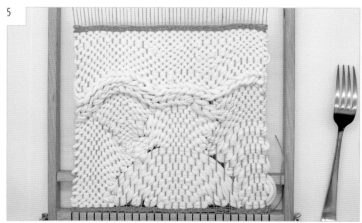

Finishing

Cutting Off the Loom

After you have woven your finishing rows, it's time to cut your piece off the loom. Sometimes when you do this it can feel that the fabric loses some of the rigidity it had when it was stretched out on the loom and under tension. This is especially true when you have a lot of free-weaving areas—this is why those last plain-weave rows are so important. But don't be disappointed. By following the next steps, your weaving will get its spark back.

Note: You can remove the heddle bar before or after the cutting off.

1. Cut off the first and last warp threads you knotted at the very beginning.

2. Unscrew and rotate the top beam toward you.

3. Unpick the warp loops from the bar's teeth.

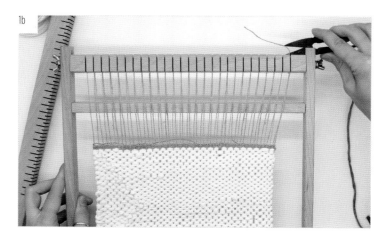

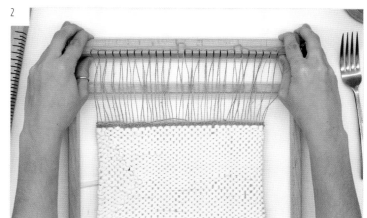

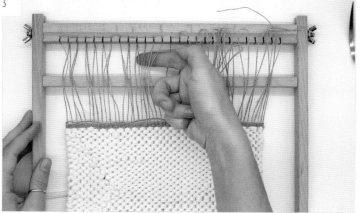

4. Gently pull your piece so as to remove the warp loops from the bottom beam.

5. Tie a knot with the loose warp ends at the bottom.

6. Hold your piece down with one hand, then pull the long top loops with your fingers in order to shorten the bottom ones—do this until they touch the weave. You just need to pull every other warp thread.

Tip: Do not pull too much, because you will shrink and squeeze your weave.

7. On free weaving—here we see the earlier project—you can follow the flow and pull according to the shapes.

8. Pick the first loop at the top and make a knot, as close as possible to the weave.

9. Carry on until you have knotted all of them.

Note: At the end you will be left with a single warp thread; tie this together with the previous loop.

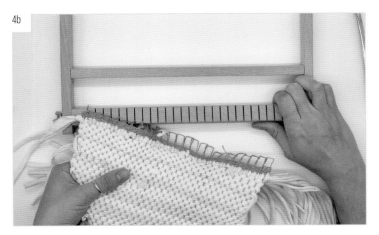

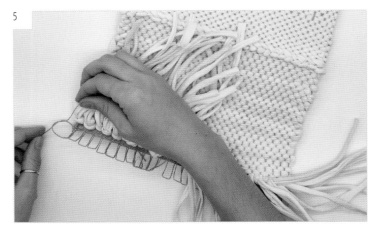

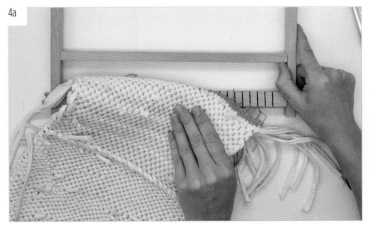

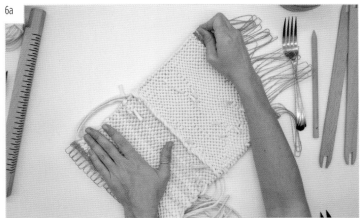

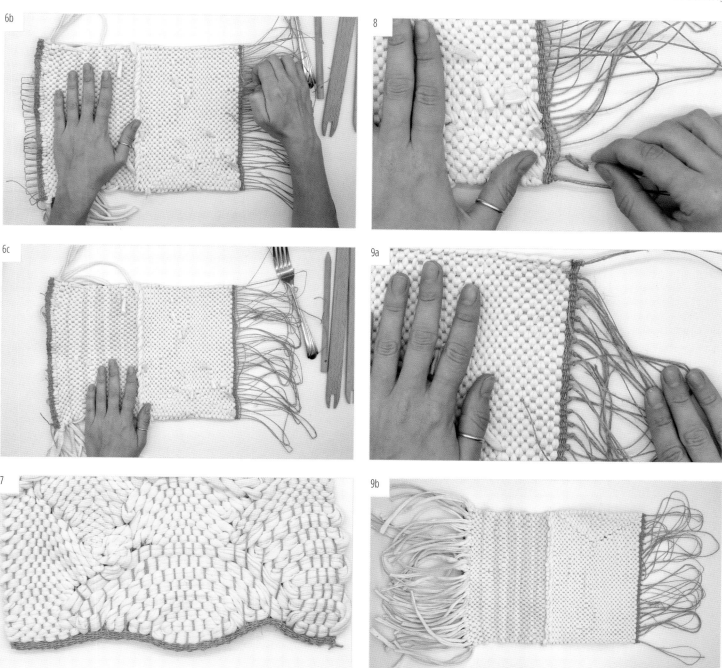

Finishing the Weave

After you've cut off your piece from the loom and secured your weave, it's time to tidy up the back.

1. If your ends on the back are long, you can chop them off a bit, but it's important that you do not trim them completely. If you do, they could work their way through to the front, where the ends will show.

2. If you want your piece to be presentable on both sides, you can hide the loose ends on the back by weaving them into the same color area, using a tapestry needle.

Hanging Your Weave (or Not)

Option 1 Using the warp threads to hang your weave

1. After you have knotted the warp loops together, cut them off at the top.

2. Attach the piece onto a nice wooden rod by double-knotting the warp threads along the top. Then just chop off any straggly ends.

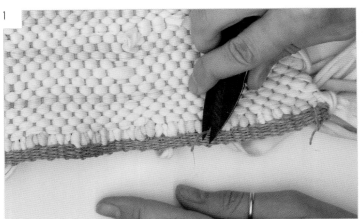

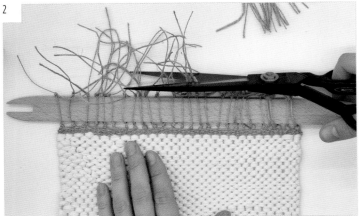

Option 2 Using a new string to hang your weave

1. After knotting the warp loops together, chop them off.

2. Cut a piece of string or yarn, about three times the width of your loom. Thread your string/yarn onto a needle. If your string/yarn is too thick to go through the needle, you can first attach a piece of thinner string to create a larger loop for the chunky yarn/string to go through.

3. Make a knot at one end of the yarn and thread through the top of your piece from the back.

4. Keeping the spacing even along the rod, continue threading every inch or two.

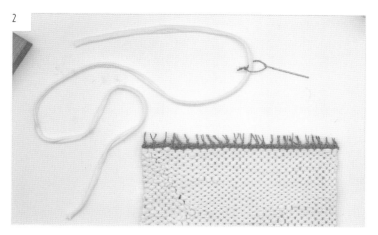

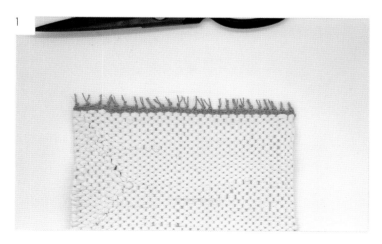

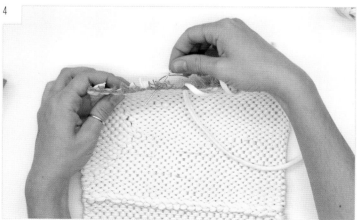

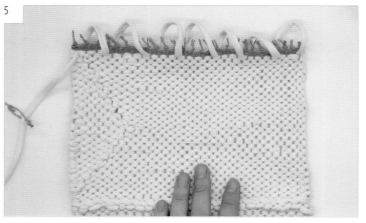

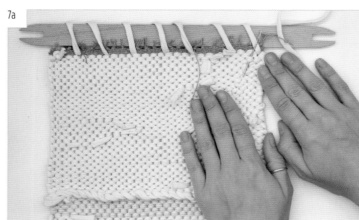

5. Leave the loops slightly loose.

6. When you have reached the other side, turn the weave over on its back and insert the hanging rod through the loops.

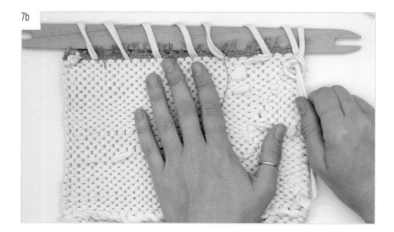

7. Tighten and even up the loops along the rod, and knot the loose end at the back (chop it off if it's too long).

And you are ready! If you don't want to hang your weave, you can just chop off the top loops—as seen here on the piece from pp. 50-54.

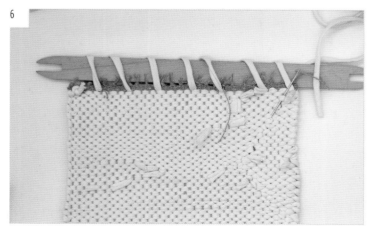

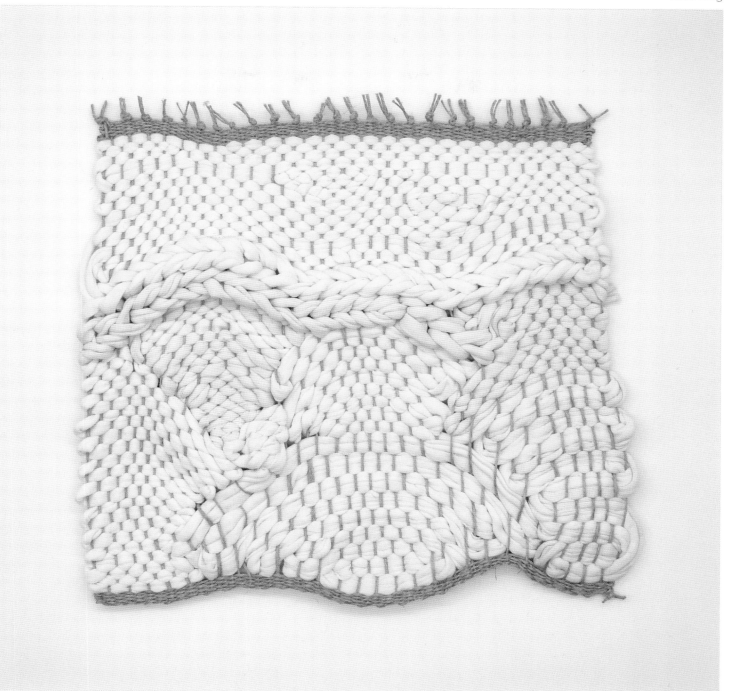

Weaving from Waste

Weaving from Waste

Creating waste is unfortunately inevitable with weaving. Even when we try to minimize it as much as possible, we all need at some point to get rid of things that have been damaged (or we no longer need) and are taking up valuable space. We have to accept that some things cannot last forever. That's why recycling is a great way to minimize the actual waste on the planet; however, we can also reuse/upcycle/repurpose some things that would have otherwise gone to waste.

Choosing Weft Yarns

Most of us have some clothes / bed linen / tablecloths / children's clothes that are so worn out that even passing them on or recycling is not an option anymore. But all such textiles are perfect to use as a weft yarn after deconstructing them—unraveling chunky knitwear—or manipulating them by cutting them into a yarn or ribbons. In addition, almost every household has ropes, strings, and gift ribbons lying around somewhere. All these can be used in your weaving as weft (or even as a warp if they are long and strong enough).

Using waste for making new things is an old technique that has been largely forgotten due to industrialization, globalization, and the mass production of cheaply and poorly made commodities. If we look back to the past, regardless of society and geographical location, most households used to weave and knit their own textiles and clothes sometimes by simply (re)using off-cuts and old clothes and fabrics. One of the many results of such a practice was that very minimal fabric went to waste, since the makers were very much aware of how much labor handcrafted garments required. One particularly noteworthy example is the traditional handwoven rag rugs for which ordinary clothes/fabric strips were used as the weft.

Weft Suggestions

- bed linen
- chunky knitwear
- jersey garments—T-shirts, dresses
- knitting yarn
- leather strings
- ribbons
- rope
- scraps of fabrics
- string
- tablecloths
- twine
- weaving yarn (rug wool thickness)
- woven garments—shirts, denim, dresses

All garments/fabrics that are in a tube format (think T-shirts, pillowcases, duvet covers, wide pants, long and straight dresses, tote bags) can be turned into a continuous yarn.

All other garments/fabrics can be cut into strips and used as ribbons. Chunky knitwear can be turned into a yarn by unraveling it.

Last, any short loose ends (knitting yarns, ribbons, strings, ropes, etc.) can be tied up together to create a new multicolor yarn. The same applies for any off-cuts or leftover yarns that you end up having from your weaving.

Making T-Shirt Yarn

You will need:
T-shirt
Scissors

1. Place your T-shirt flat on a table and cut off the sleeve top area from armpit to armpit all the way around.

2. Cut off the (waistband) seam at the bottom of T-shirt.

Important: Do not discard your cut-offs. These will be useful as fillers (see pp. 74–75), to start your weaving farther up your loom.

3. Stretch and flatten down the rest of the T-shirt. It's easy to turn the tube now. Fold twice horizontally, but leave about 1.5 in. overlapping at the top.

4. Cut 1 in. wide strips straight across the T-shirt.

Important: Do not cut all the way to the top. Stop where the folding area stops.

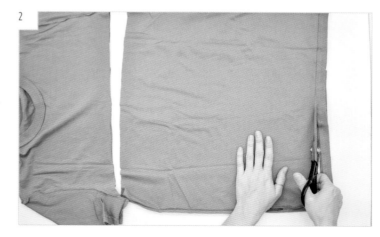

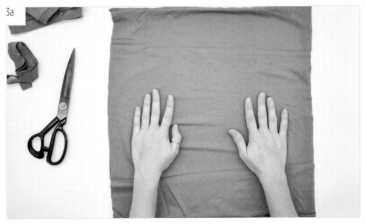

3a

4a

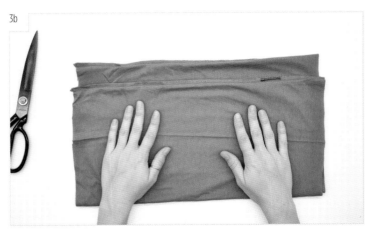

3b

4b

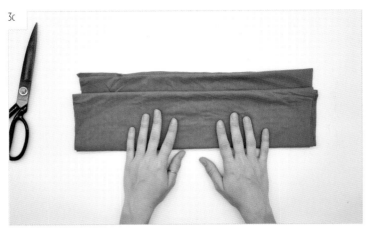

3c

4c

5. Unfold the T-shirt and drape it over your hand. Put the scissors into the first cut in the front and cut off the first strip.

6. Place the scissors into the next cut on the front and cut diagonally to meet the first cut at the back.

7. Repeat, cutting diagonally from one slit into the front of the next one at the back until you reach the end.

8. Insert your scissors into the last slit from the outside edge and cut it off.

You should now have a continuous long flat strip of fabric.

9. To make it into a lovely, stretchy, rounded yarn, grip one end of the strip and start tugging hard while wrapping it into a ball. Carry on until you have tugged and wound the entire length.

Your T-shirt yarn is ready to be woven!

5a

5b

5c

6

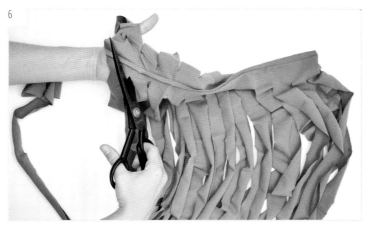

9a

7

9b

8

Making Pillowcase Yarn

You will need:
Pillowcase
Scissors

1. Flatten the pillowcase onto an even surface and smooth it out. Cut off the seams at both ends to create a tube. If your pillowcase has an inner flap, simply cut this out at each side seam. Keep the off-cuts.

2. Fold it twice horizontally, leaving about 1.5 in. overlapping at the top.

3. Cut 1 in. wide strips straight across the pillowcase.

Important: Do not cut all the way to the top—stop at the overlap.

4. Unfold the pillowcase and drape it over your hand, put the scissors into the first cut in the front, and cut off the first strip.

5. Place the scissors into the next cut at the front and cut diagonally to meet the first cut at the back.

6. Repeat cutting diagonally from the front slit into the next one at the back until you reach the end.

7. Insert your scissors into the last slit from the outside edge and cut it off.

You should now have a continuous long flat strip of fabric.

8. Grip one end of the strip and wind it into a ball. Carry on until you wind the whole length. Your pillowcase-ribbon yarn is ready to be used.

Tip: This technique is suitable for any tube-shaped clothing or household item.

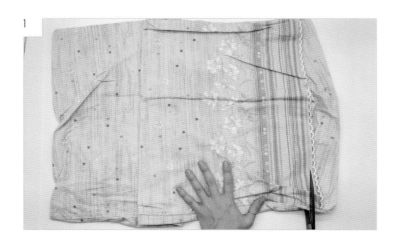

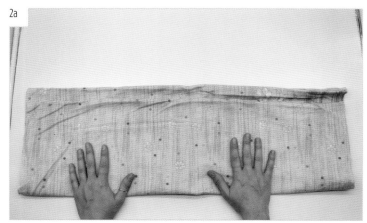

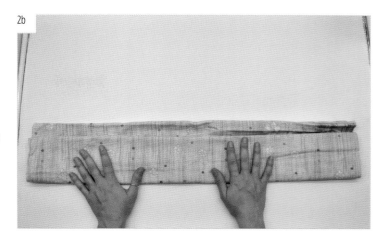

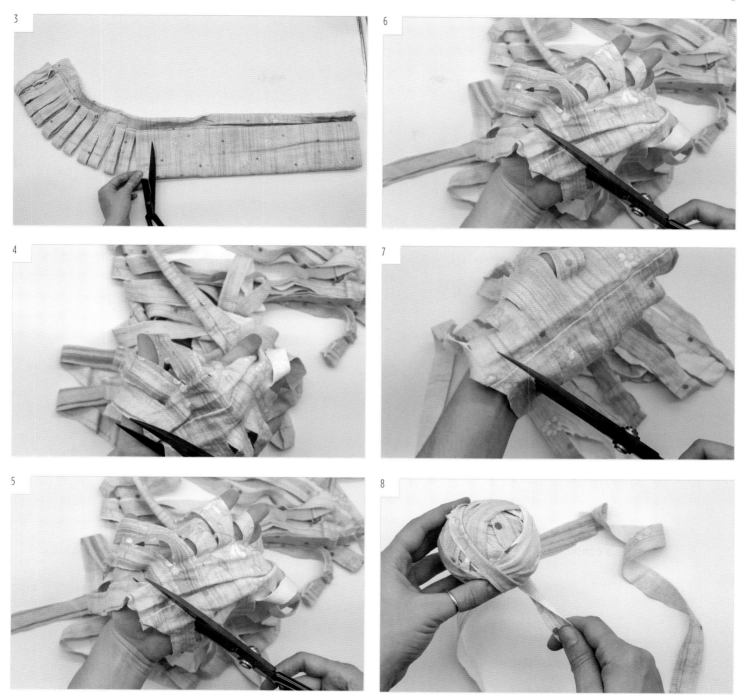

3

4

5

6

7

8

Table Mat

This table or place mat design is based on vertical stripes that are made by alternatively weaving with two colors. Since I am using quite chunky T-shirt yarns, my table mat will have a polka dot texture.

Feel free to experiment with different thicknesses of yarns and textures. Remember, though, that you need to use yarns of the same thickness for each table mat in order for the vertical stripes to be created.

You will need:
Frame loom (with heddle bar)
82 ft. (25 m) warp thread (linen)
3 same-thickness colored yarns (T-shirt yarns)
Fork
Scissors
2 shuttles
Snip scissors
Tapestry needle

Tips

• I like to use a natural undyed linen warp thread to give a more organic feeling to my place mat.

• For the weft colors, I advise you to select one muted color (as the base color), and two contrasting brighter ones.

• The selections and proportions of colors are only a suggestion—feel free to experiment with your own color palette and combinations.

1. Warp your loom and place the heddle bar in position. Remember to check your tension along the way.

2. Because I want both the top and bottom sides of my table mat to look the same regarding the finishing knots of the warp threads, I started weaving a bit higher up the loom than usual. This was so as to leave a bit of extra length at the bottom warp loops to make knotting easier afterward.

To do this, before starting weaving, I wove in a chunky piece of waste fabric from the T-shirt yarn. This will be removed when the weave is complete, so the color doesn't matter.

3. Weave some rows with warp thread—about a quarter of an inch. Remembering to create the curve (see p. 30).

4. Take your muted color of yarn (I've used brown) and one of the bright colors (green) and wind up your shuttles.

5. Weave one row with your base color (here the brown yarn from the right-hand side). Remember to leave a tail of about 2 inches.

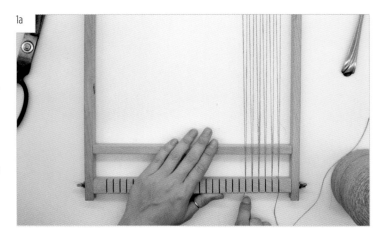

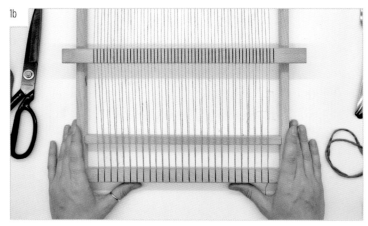

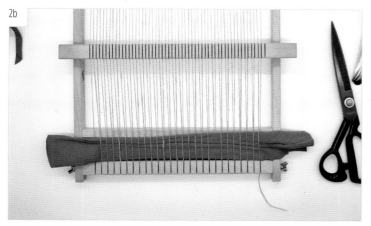

2b

3c

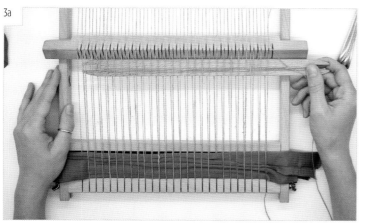

3a

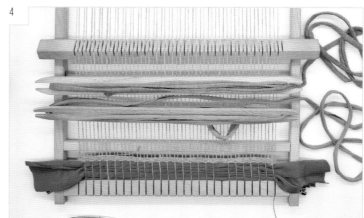

4

3b

5

6. Without cutting off the base yarn (brown), weave the other color (green) by starting it from the opposite side (here from the left-hand side). Remember to leave a tail 2 inches long.

7. Weave one row with base color (brown) and weave in the loose tail from the first row.

By changing color on every row, you cover only the odd warps with that color and the even warps with the other color, thus creating unwoven edges. To avoid this, it's important to make sure that—for both colors on every row—your weaving yarn goes under the yarn of the previous row at the edges, so it will be "locked" in. (Here on the left-hand side, the brown yarn goes under the green.)

8. Weave a row with the other color (green) and weave in the tail of the second row. Remember to lock in the edge.

9. Carry on alternating the two colors. Remember to beat down your weft as your design progresses.

10. When you have woven approximately a third of your piece, cut off the bright color (green) and replace it with the other one (blue). Since your tail will show if you weave it in as usual, you can instead go around the first warp thread and then follow the exact path of the previous row.

11. Carry on weaving by alternating the base color (brown) with the other bright color (blue) so a band of color is created.

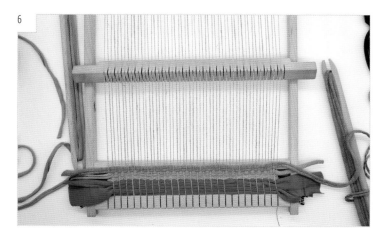

7c

9b

8
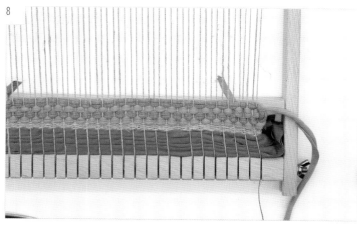

10
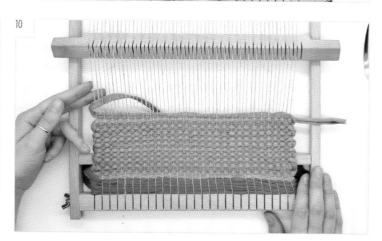

9a
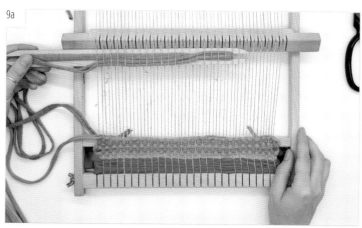

11
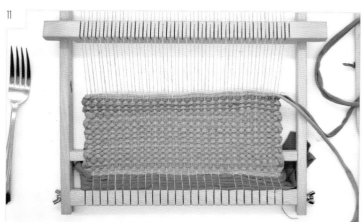

12. Continue weaving again with the first bright color (green) and the base (brown).

Tip: If you change the sequence of the colors by skipping one row, so there are two rows of the same color together—here with the brown—you are "moving" the stripes widthwise on the warp.

13. When you have woven a bit more than half your piece, change the bright color again (from green to blue) and carry on alternating it with your base yarn.

14. When you have woven a larger band of color than the base and the second bright color (blue) together, return to using the first bright color (green), then your base again.

15. Weave on for a few rows and then change again back to the other bright color (blue) and weave until you reach the top of the loom.

Tip: In order to weave the maximum length possible on the loom, you can—if you want—remove the heddle bar and continue weaving without it.

12a

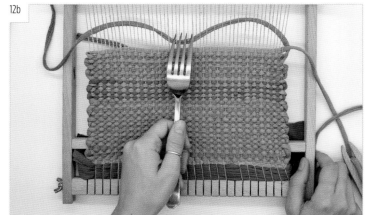

12b

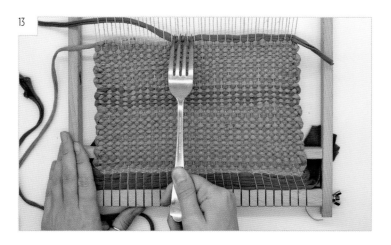

13

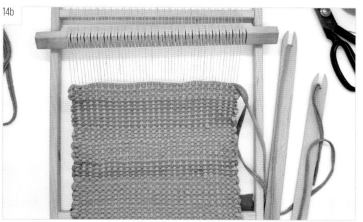

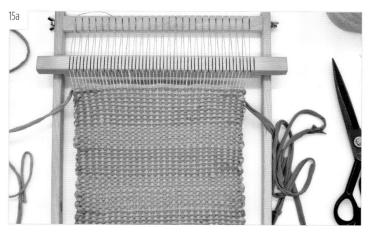

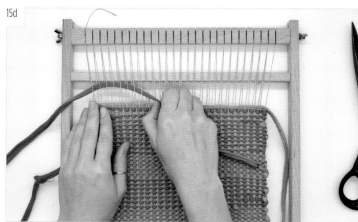

16. When you have reached the top (just before the horizontal wooden stick of the loom), finish your piece with a few rows of plain weave, using the warp thread.

17. Remove the strip of fabric from the bottom of the loom.

18. Cut your piece off the loom and knot the warp threads across both the bottom and top. Trim the threads to the desired length to form your fringe.

19. Last, tidy up the back and weave in any loose wefts.

Your table mat is ready.

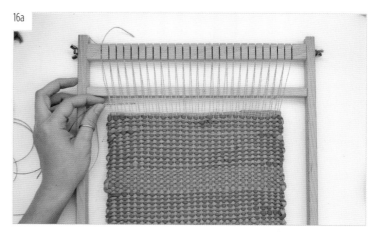

16a

16b

17

18a

19

18b

18c

Clutch Bag

This an easy project to make. Depending on the size of your loom, you can weave anything from a small wallet or makeup bag to a large laptop case. Note that stitching or sewing skills are required for this piece.

You will need:
Frame loom (with heddle bar)
82 ft. (25 m) warp thread (cotton knitting yarn)

2 muted-color yarns (T-shirt yarn), for the base color
1 or 2 bright-colored yarns (Sari yarn)
1 textured/fluffy yarn
1 cotton/linen rope
Fork
Piece of fabric (off-cut) for lining (optional)
Sewing thread
2 shuttles
Snips scissors
Stitching needle (or sewing machine)
Tapestry needle
Zipper

Tip: For this project, I have chosen a cotton crochet yarn (1 mm lace weight) since I wanted to match my warp to my zipper, and also to use a softer material than the traditional cotton warp thread. You can use any warp thread yarn you like—but remember that it needs to be strong.

1. Warp your loom and place the heddle bar in position. Remember to check your tension as you thread it up.

2. Weave the starting row with your warp thread.

3. Weave a few rows with one of the base colors and then introduce the other base color.

4. Carry on weaving alternate vertical stripes (see Table Mat project).

5. After you have woven a few rows, weave in one row of rope. Leave the tails out on both sides.

6. Now weave alternate rows of bright color and textured/fluffy yarn to create a band of color. When this is done, insert another row of rope, leaving tails on both sides.

7. Return to weaving alternate rows of both base colors.

8. When you have woven about two-thirds of your woven area, insert another single row of rope—leaving the tails loose on both sides.

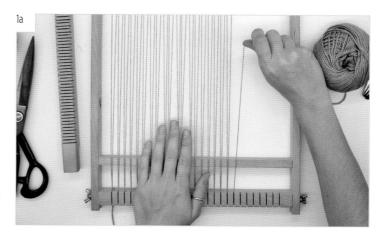

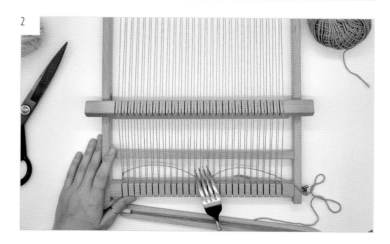

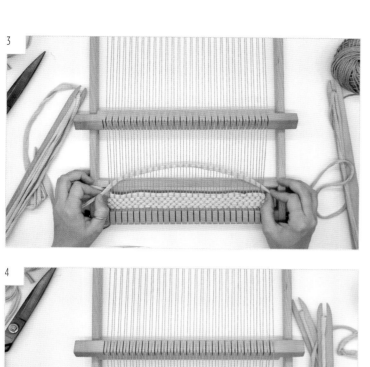

3

6

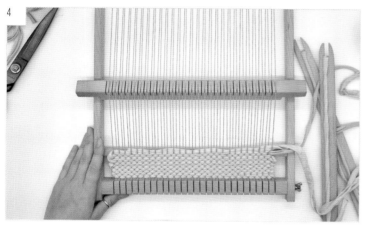

4

7

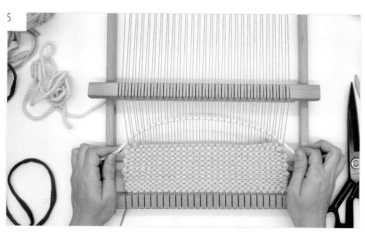

5

8

9. Weave a larger band of color than before with the other (or same) bright color and the textured/fluffy yarn.

10. Insert a row of rope, again leaving tails at either end.

11. Carry on weaving with both base colors up to the top.

12. Finish with a section of warp thread rows.

13. Take your piece off the loom, pull the bottom loops in, and knot the top ones.

14. Chop off the warp loops and any loose weft ends on the back, and place the lining fabric (if you are using one) on top of the back (inner) side.

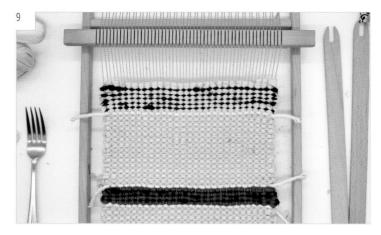

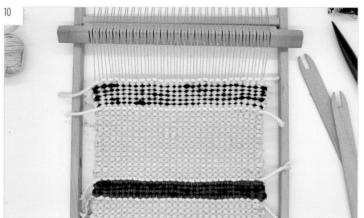

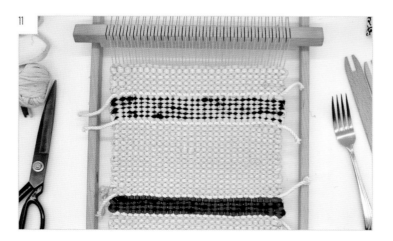

12

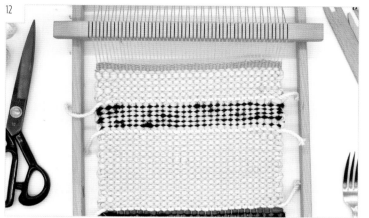

13c

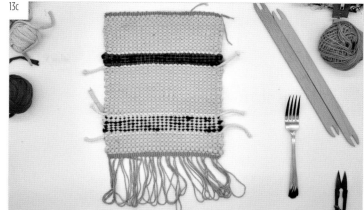

13a

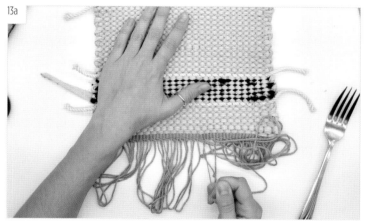

14a

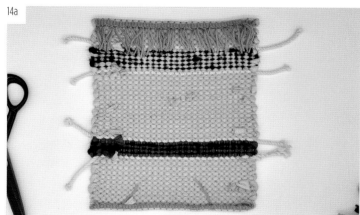

13b

14b

15. Use pins to attach the zipper in position between the woven piece and the lining fabric.

16. Stitch the first zipper edge by hand or with a sewing machine. Fold your purse in half so the top edges meet. Sew the other side to the zipper. Then sew your side seams. Be sure to attach the zipper between the woven piece and the lining fabric accordingly.

17. Last, unravel the rope ends and chop them short to create tassels. Add a piece of rope to the zip for easy access.

Enjoy your new bag!

16a

15a

16b

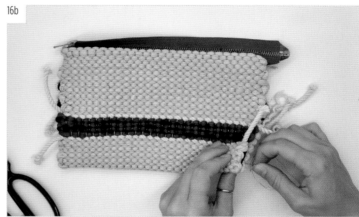

15b

17

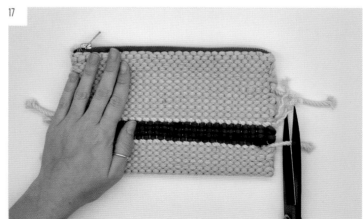

Wall Hanging with a Fringe

This is a free-weaving project, so gather a few yarns that you like to create your color palette, and decide what you want to use as you go. Most likely you will not use them all!

(Highly recommended: Put on your favorite music and let the mood guide you.)

You will need:
Frame loom (with heddle bar)
82 ft. (25 m) warp thread (kitchen twine)
4 to 6 colored yarns (T-shirt yarn, recycled linen, knitting wool yarns)
Fork
Scissors
2 shuttles
Snips scissors
Tapestry needle

Tips

• *Since this project requires free weaving, it's quite likely that your warp will be more visible than usual. That's why I have chosen to use a colored thread (black and white cotton twine) to give a marl effect to the piece.*

• *I want to add a fringe/tassels at the end of the piece, but I'm not going to start with it, since I want to see which of my yarns looks most effective in the weave—allowing me to use the same in my fringe. Also, I want my fringe to follow the flow of the free weaving, and then to hide the knots of the top warp loops underneath it.*

1. Warp your loom and place the heddle bar in position.

2. Weave a few rows with the warp thread—about a quarter of an inch.

3. Choose one of your yarns (the thinner one if there's a choice) to be your base yarn—this can be used to plain-weave any "empty" areas in between the free weaving to add some rigidity. Weave a few rows with it before starting your free weaving, so it doesn't look odd when it's added in later on.

4. Start creating free-weaving shapes by mixing together two yarns (see pp. 50–54.)

5. Use a bright color to fill small areas.

Note: You might need to weave and unweave before you decide which colors and textures work best next to each other. It is part of the process (and nobody will ever know).

6. Carry on playing around with shapes and curves until you are happy with the effect.

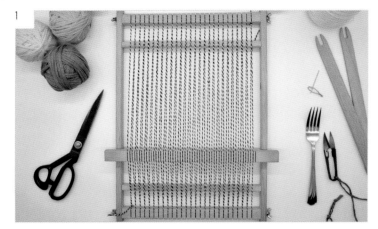

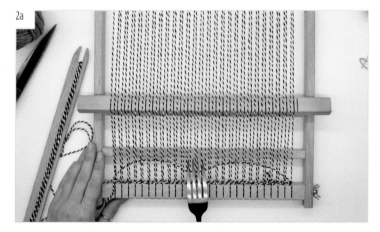

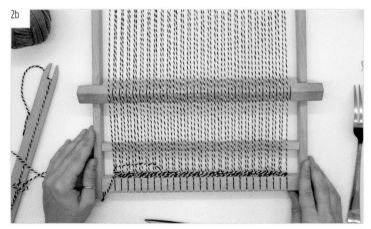

3

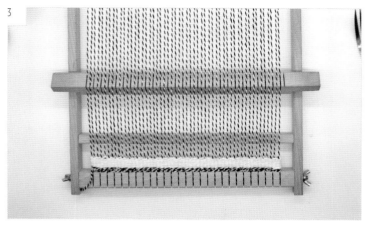

6

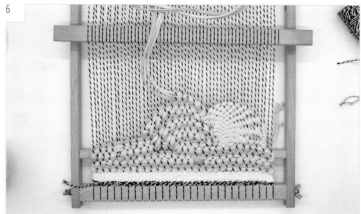

4

5

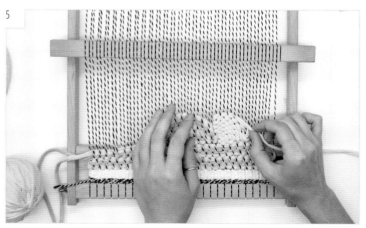

7. You can start adding some plain weave by using your background color on any small unwoven areas or at the sides (or both). Remember to beat down your weft as your design progresses.

8. Introduce a new color and carry on free weaving.

9. Weave in a small area of the bright colors again on the other side of the piece to create a more balanced composition.

10. You can also weave regular rows across the full width and follow the flow in order to create wavy lines.

11. Weave a row of braid to add some texture to the project.

Tip: Leave the ends hanging at the sides to add a bit of a movement.

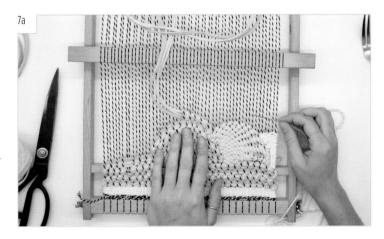

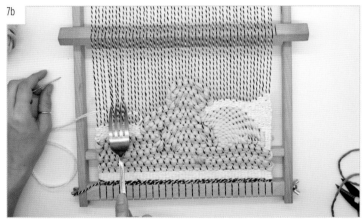

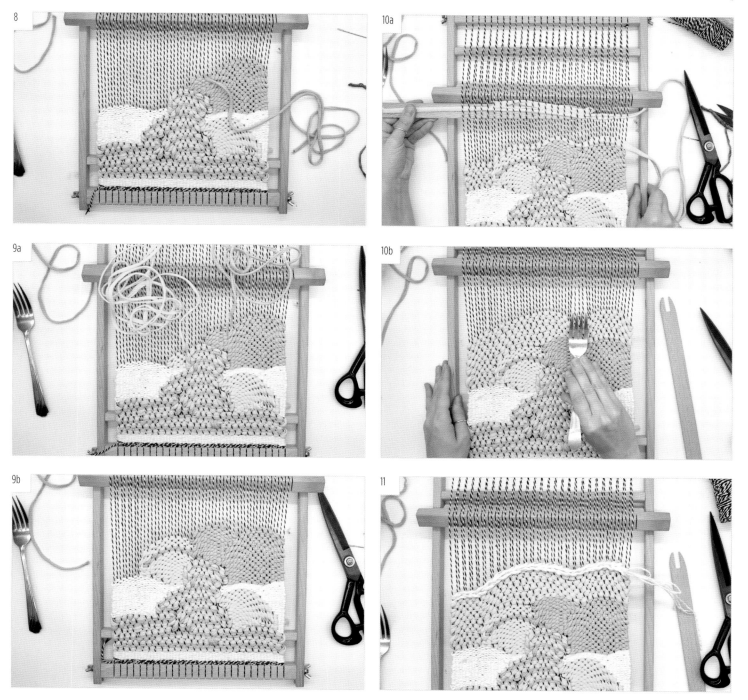

12. Carry on weaving until you reach the top.

Tip: Finish your piece with the least used color (but not the brightest one) together with your background color to add some balance to your piece.

13. Turn your loom so the heddle bar is at the bottom, and remove it. Now it's time to add your fringe/tassels, before weaving the final rows with the warp thread. Trim the ends of the tassels at the bottom by following the flow of your weaving.

Tip: For the fringe/tassels, remember to use all the yarns you've used in the weave (though not necessarily the background color). Use the brightest color least.

14. You can add a second layer of tassels underneath to add extra richness and texture. I recommend using the background color for these.

15. When you have finished with the tassel/fringing, weave the finishing rows by using a tapestry needle with your warp yarns.

16. Last, after you have cut the weaving off the loom, pull and knot your warp threads. Use a tapestry needle to hide the top loose warp thread at the back.

You can now hang your piece on the wall (see pp. 58–61).

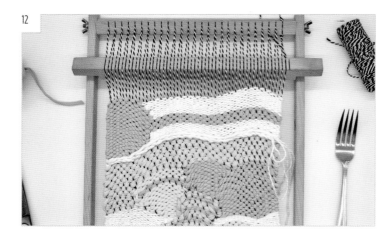

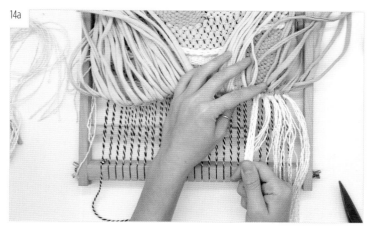

14a

15b

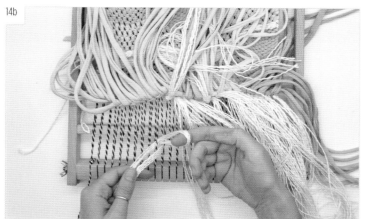

14b

15a

16

Weaving
on a Circular
Frame Loom

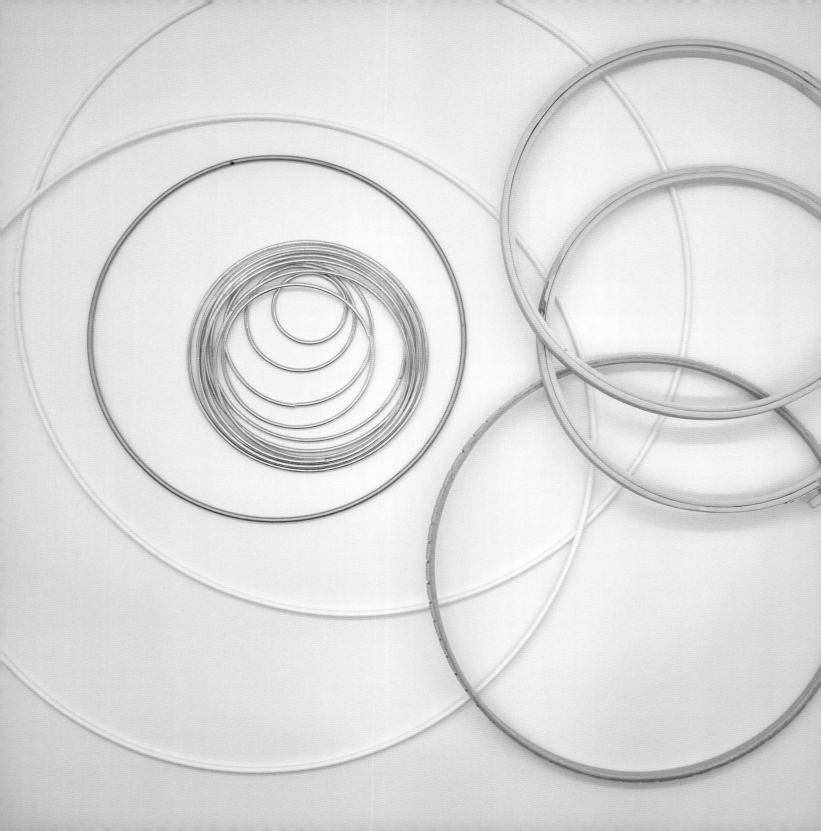

Weaving on a Circular Frame Loom

Circular weaving, as the name suggests, is a great way to weave round pieces. However, weaving circular shapes on a frame loom is pretty tricky: the solution is just to use a round frame. The weaving itself is exactly the same—you need to go over and under and vice versa, and you can use regular-weave (tapestry-like) or free-weaving techniques. Depending on the size of your circular frame, you can make wall hangings, cushions covers, bags, rugs, table mats, and many, many more things. The options and styles are endless; just let your imagination guide you.

You can use any circular frame as a loom (embroidery hoop, Hula-Hoop, lighting frame, picture/mirror frame, etc.) or you can purchase a ready-made circular loom. The only difference between a ready-made circular loom to a DIY one is that the former has predetermined places (teeth or pegs) to space the warp evenly. But you can easily do this yourself. If you are experimenting with different thicknesses of weft yarn, it can be better to have the option of choosing the spacing of the warp threads according to the weft that you are using to weave.

When you're choosing a frame, keep in mind that if you are making a wall piece, it might be more practical to weave your piece on the same frame you are planning to hang it. In that way, you are skipping one step and won't lose any of your piece's tension and spark.

Designing Your Piece (or Not)

As with rectangular-frame weaving, before you start weaving on your circular frame, it is useful—but not necessary—to have a rough idea of what you are making.

If you want to preplan your weaving, the first step is to choose the right size of frame, depending on what you would like to make. The second and very important step is to choose wisely the yarns for the warp and weft, in terms of fibers, thickness, and texture. Then choose your colors in order to create your color palette.

It's up to you how much detail you want to go into when planning your piece. Otherwise, you can just gather together a colorful variety of yarns and materials that inspire you, and let your mood and imagination do the rest.

The important thing is to get started and try to translate whatever you have in your mind into your weave. It might end up being completely different from your initial idea (this often happens), but it could be something brilliant that you are thrilled with and didn't expect!

The more you weave, the more familiar you'll get with the practice itself, and the accompanying equipment/tools and materials. Also, it will become easier to make exactly what you had in mind in the first place.

Choosing Yarns

Choosing a Warp Thread

When it comes to choosing the warping thread, weaving on a circular loom is exactly the same as rectangular-frame weaving. The yarn should be strong and smooth and able to withstand the friction and stretching created by the weaving action. Try to avoid fancy yarns that have very little twist, since they will be more prone to breakage.

The biggest difference is that for circular weaving, your warp will be much more visible than on frame weaving, so you might want to choose a colored thread.

Last, depending on what you are making, you can choose the thickness of your warp thread—a fine one for small pieces (such as cushions, bags, art) and a thicker one for rugs and large wall pieces. You'll know which one works best only after you have tried a few, so experiment and find out which works for you.

Warp Suggestions

• 3-4 ply (1 mm) cotton/linen string
• baker's (cotton marl) twine
• butcher's (rayon) twine
• crochet (cotton/bamboo) lace weight yarn
• flax/sisal twine
• gardening/craft (jute) twine

Choosing Weft Yarns

Exactly the same rules apply for choosing a weft yarn for circular weaving as for frame weaving. Feel free to experiment and try different fibers and materials, and use waste as much as you can (see "Weaving from Waste").

Weft Suggestions

• bed linen
• chunky knitwear
• jersey garments (T-shirts, dresses)
• knitting yarn
• leather string
• ribbon
• rope
• scraps of fabric
• string
• tablecloths
• tea towels
• twine
• woven garments (shirts, denim, dresses)

If you are using an embroidery hoop, remove the outer ring and set it to one side for later use.

1. Tie (double-knot) your warp thread around one of the slits in the ring.

2. Pull the warp thread straight across the hoop.

3. Bring the warp thread over the hoop and then down and around. Pull the warp thread back toward the center, into the next slit, about 1 inch along on the right-hand side, where the warp thread started with a knot.

Note: You are making a figure eight, so that the warp threads meet in the middle.

4. Working clockwise, continue to bring the warp threads across the loom to the slits beside the previous thread. You will always be passing the thread over an edge and then around to the bottom, then over the next slit.

Important: Keep a good tension, but not too tight, because otherwise your frame will distort.

Warping

How to warp any circular (or oval) frame loom

You will need:
Circular weaving loom. If you don't have a circular loom, you
   can use an embroidery hoop. However, it won't have slits,
   and you'll have to make these yourself. Warping without slits
   can be done but is difficult.
Scissors
Tapestry needle
Warp thread (amount depends on the size of the hoop)

1

4a

2

4b

3

4c

5. Continue working around the frame with your figure eights until you are left with the last two empty slits.

6. Cut your warp thread, but make sure you have more than enough to finish warping—you'll need a bit more than twice the diameter of your frame.

7. Thread the tapestry needle with the long warp thread tail.

8. At this point you'll see that the center is a messy crisscross of warps. Taking your needle with the warp thread, go around the second-to-last slit as normal and then pull it through the center and down and around between the warp threads. You'll instantly see that the warps even out to nice triangles.

9. Now loop your warp thread around the last slit on the frame and go once again through the central warp meeting point.

10. Pull the yarn and take it back to the first slit and tie it together.

Note: If you are using an embroidery hoop, you can now put the outer hoop around the warped hoop and tighten it, so that your warp threads don't slide around.

You are ready to weave!

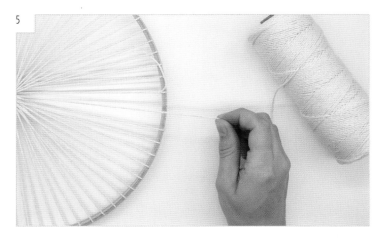

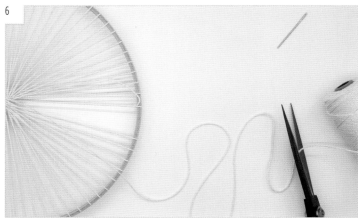

8a

9b
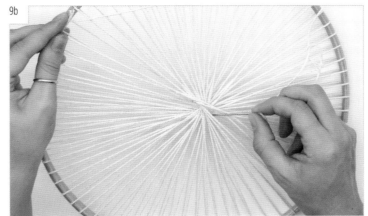

8b

10a

9a
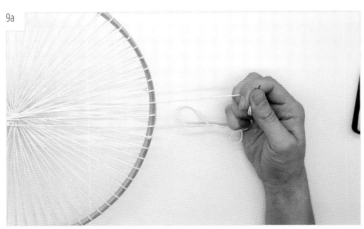

10b
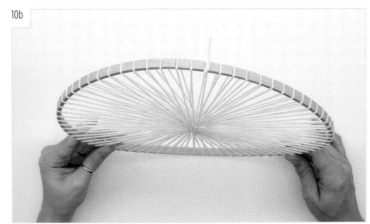

Weaving

Weaving on a circular frame is the same process as weaving on an ordinary (rectangular/square) frame, whether you do regular (tapestry) weaving or free weaving.

Tapestry Weaving

If you are weaving using traditional tapestry techniques, the only differences are that you are building your piece from the center outward, and that your rows are added in a spiral format. Experiment with different weaving sequences apart from ordinary plain weave, such as twill: going over two warp threads and under one. See the Fringed Cushion project.

It's still advisable to start off your piece with some plain-weave rows, since this will help keep your warp even and aligned. Use a thin weft yarn, because the warp threads in the center are very close together—you can change to gradually thicker yarns as you weave outward toward the frame. For once it's not necessary to start with your warp thread, although you can. However, it is still advisable to end your weaving with a few rows of the warp thread to even up your piece (both for aesthetic and tension reasons).

Free Weaving

If you are free weaving, you don't necessarily have to start from the center. You can instead set up your warp as a "net" and freely create shapes—this works particularly well if you're not planning to remove your piece from the frame upon completion.

Plain Weave

1. Thread the weft into a tapestry needle and start weaving an inch or so out from the center. Because the warp threads are jumbled and very close to each other, it's much easier to start weaving higher up on the warp threads and then push your weft down to the center with a fork.

2. Carry on weaving, changing colors and thicknesses as you go. In order to change weft yarn, just leave a short tail hanging loose at the back and start your next yarn with a bit of overlap.

Color Blocks and Shapes

3. Weaving color blocks and shapes on a circular loom is the same as on the frame loom, and you still work plain weaving into the smaller areas. Be aware, though, that these shapes will not have the same dimensions on every side, since the warp threads have different spacing across the loom.

1a

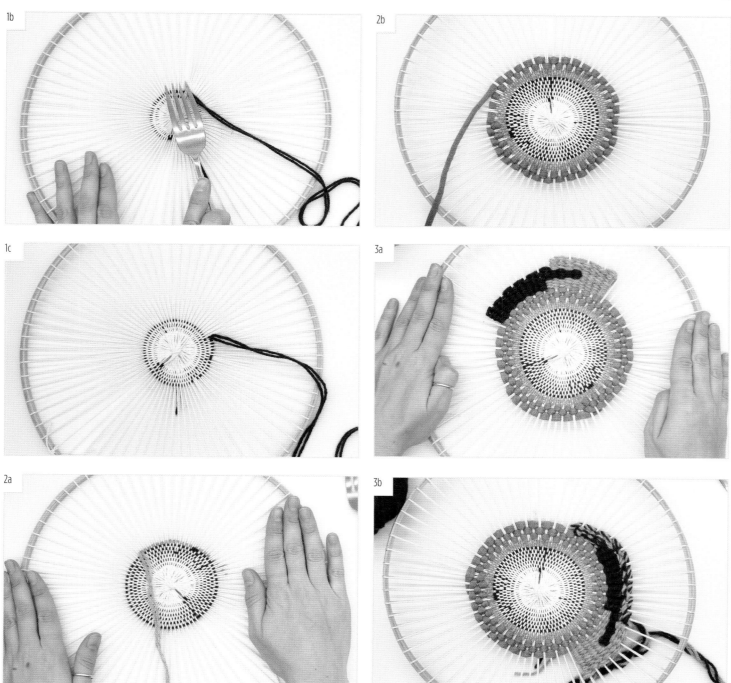

Finishing

Cutting Off the Loom

1. When you've finished and woven some plain-weave rows with warp thread, it's time to cut your piece off the loom. Sometimes, at this point the weave loses some of its rigidity, because it's no longer under tension. This is especially true of free weaving, or when a lot of chunky weft yarns have been used—that's why the last plain-weave rows are really important. Don't be disappointed; this can be rectified. Cut off the warp threads and make paired knots as close as possible to your last weft row. Chop off the warp ends if you need to.

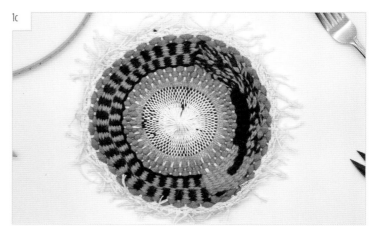

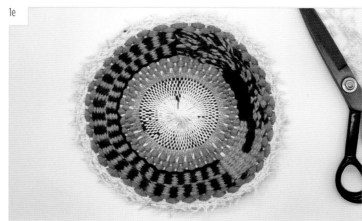

Finishing the Weave

2. Whether or not you are going to cut your piece off the loom or keep it on the frame, you need to clean up any long, loose weft ends from the back of your weave.

If the back won't be visible, still make sure you trim any loose weft ends—but not too short. Or weave them in if you want the back side to be neat and presentable.

As a final touch, when you're keeping the piece on the frame you can cover the frame itself to complement your weaving. Either wrap the frame with a contrasting yarn or attach tassels to it—just around the lower edge, or right the way around.

Wrapping the frame

You can wrap the entire frame with one or more colors, or just a portion of it (see pp. 132–133).

Adding tassels to the frame

You can add short tassels all around the frame or just add long ones at the base. See "Making a Fringe/Tassels" (pp. 34–37). This shows how to add tassels on a single warp thread, but instead of using the warps you knot them onto the frame.

Hanging your weave

If you have kept your piece on the frame, it's easy to hang it up. You can attach it to the wall directly with a nail or hook, or hang it from a piece of string or ribbon.

If you've cut the weave off the loom and you want to hang it on the wall, depending on its size and weight, you can hang it from some string or yarn. Alternatively, attach it to something solid, such as a piece of wood or cork tile, or stitch it onto a piece of firm fabric and then frame the fabric.

Fringed Cushion

With this project I decided to upcycle an old pair of denim pants, so my color palette was blue based. I chose materials and yarns to match the denim—blue, navy, black, gray, and white. Additionally, because the meeting point of the warp threads would be visible, I chose a black-and-white cotton twine for contrast.

With your project, feel free to experiment with different yarns, fibers, and textures. Just remember that you will need thin yarns for the inner center, then chunkier yarns as you weave outward toward the ring.

With the following steps you'll be making a circular cushion top with fringe. You will then need to stitch it onto a cushion cover and fill it with an inner pad.

Depending on the inner filling, the cushion could be for a round stool or for your sofa or bed. However, using the same instructions, you could instead make a wall hanging—either cutting it off the loom or keeping it on.

You will need:

Circular frame loom—minimum 2 in. larger than the
  cushion cover
2 colored thin knitting yarns
Cotton twine for the warp (kitchen twine)
Denim yarn—made out of pants
Fabric strips—extra chunky (fabric off-cuts)
Fork
2 natural medium-thickness wool rug yarn
Scissors
T-shirt yarn—chunky
Tapestry needle

Weaving needle

1. Warp your ring frame with the cotton twine. Keep a good tension—not too tight but definitely not too loose. I have deliberately placed the meeting point of the warp threads a bit off-center to make the project more interesting.

2. Using your tapestry needle, thread one of your thick yarns (here, navy blue) and start weaving at the center. Remember to beat down the weave as you progress with your design.

Tip: Because of the large diameter of the ring, you will end up with lots of warp threads, so think of every loop (two threads) as one warp.

3. After you've woven a few rows, change to your other thin yarn (I've used black) and weave a few rows with it until the spacing in between the warp loops obviously increases.

4. Then, with your medium-thickness yarn (here, light-gray rug wool), weave a few rows—similar to the total rows of the two previous yarns.

You can add some more texture to the piece by weaving in a different sequence: over two, under one—this creates a twill weave pattern that adds extra contrast.

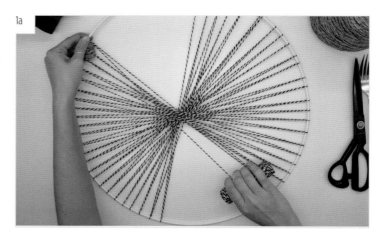

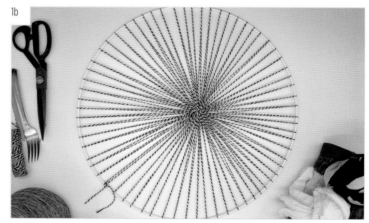

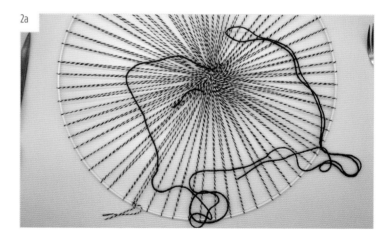

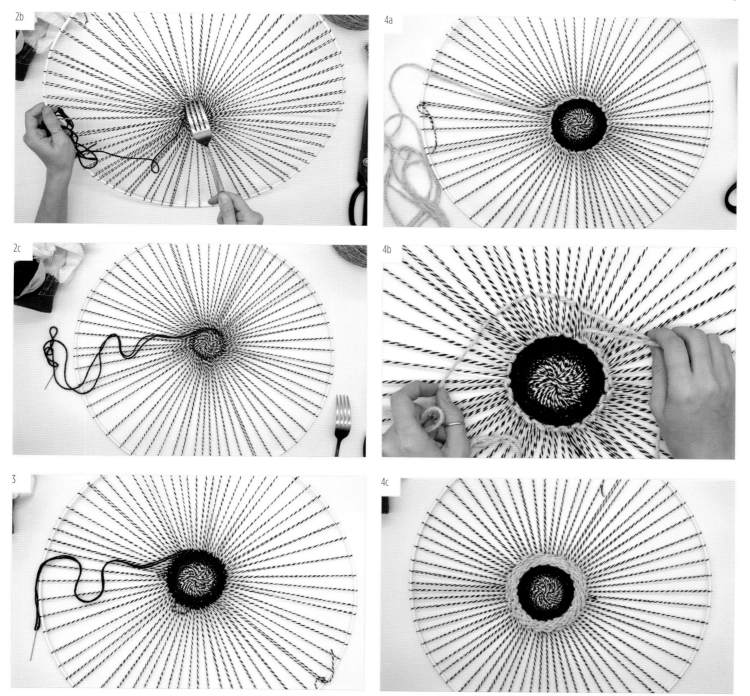

2b

4a

2c

4b

3

4c

5. After you've cut your denims into a yarn of about 1 in. thick (see pp. 66–69, "Making T-Shirt Yarn"), weave a few rows with it.

Tip: Make sure your yarn is nice and flat before starting.

6. Continue using T-shirt yarn—this time in ecru.

7. Now to add some texture. Start making a few rows of braid (Rya knots, pp. 53–54) with the yarns you used at the very beginning of your weave (here, navy blue and black). You can double or triple up (or more) the lengths of your thin yarn, so you end up with a nice fluffy braid.

Tip: I use a tapestry needle to make Rya knots. If the yarn is a bit too chunky to easily get through the needle, I use an extra loop of warp cotton and thread the yarn through that.

8. I added an extra row of braid to the larger area of the circle to even up the off-center circles a bit (use gray rug wool).

9. Add one more row of braid with a slightly thinner yarn to tighten everything up together (use light-gray rug wool).

Tip: Change the direction of the braid to play around with the texture.

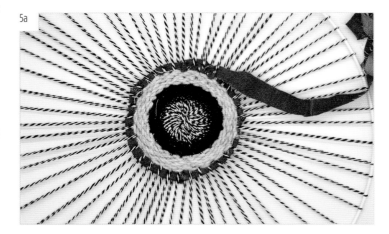

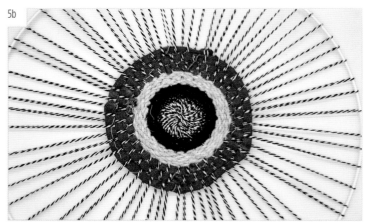

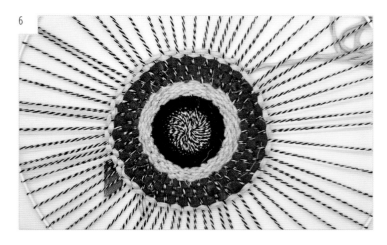

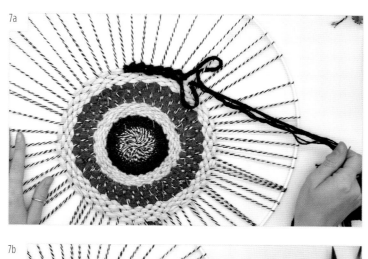

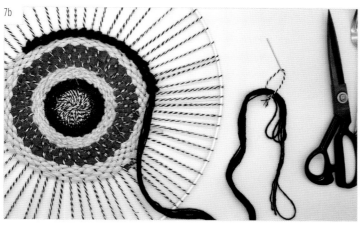

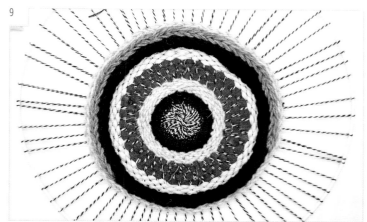

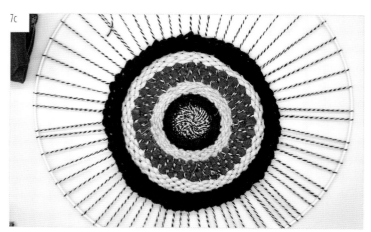

10. Weave a few rows with T-shirt yarn (here, ecru) to give a bit of firmness to your piece and to brighten it up a bit.

11. Weave a few rows with the denim yarn. This time beat it down a bit more to give it a different texture—so it looks squeezed rather than flat.

12. Weave in a chunky strip of fabric (use white) for about two-thirds of the circle: this will even up the piece.

Tip: You can add a bit of texture by making a knot (around the warp loop) at one end of the fabric. Make sure it is not too chunky if you're making a stool cushion.

13. Weave a few rows with thin yarns (this time I've used black) to complete the circle. Make an odd number of rows. This will even up the plain weave.

14. Weave one full circle row with your fabric strips (here I've used navy blue / ecru).

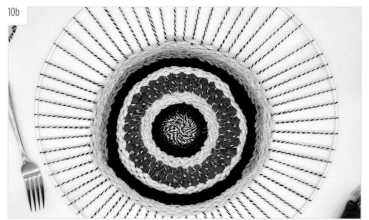

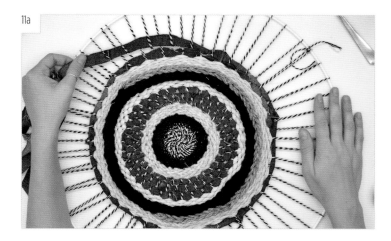

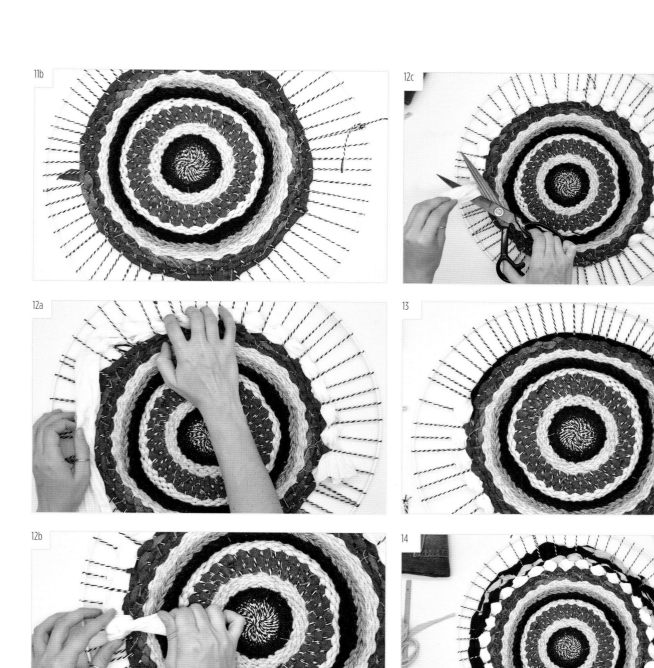

11b

12c

12a

13

12b

14

15. Continue to weave as many rows as you need with the T-shirt yarn (ecru) to finish up your piece.

Note: It's a good idea to use a T-shirt yarn for this part, because it is very elastic and can squeeze more at the narrow bottom area. This will even up the weave since it can spread in the space and compress where there's less room.

16. Time to cut the piece off the ring. Because I wanted to take maximum advantage of my weaving area, there's not much left of the warp strings to use to tie together and secure the weft. So I used an alternative method.

Start by separating the warp loops into pairs. If a single warp is left over, add it to one of the pairs.

17. Each warp pair consists of two loops, so four threads (apart from the last one, which has six threads). With the warp string and needle, weave three rows through each of the pairs—as close as possible to the last weft row.

18. Pull the ends very tight.

19. Flip the piece over and tie a double knot.

20. Repeat for all the warp pairs.

21. Cut the piece off the loom.

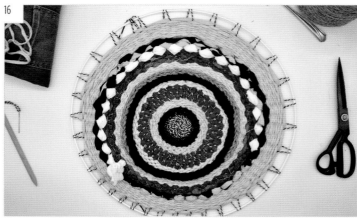

18

21a

19

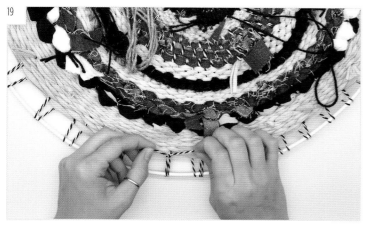

21b

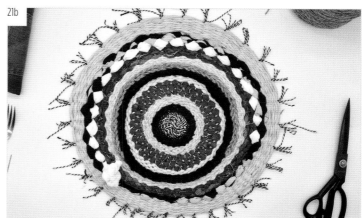

20

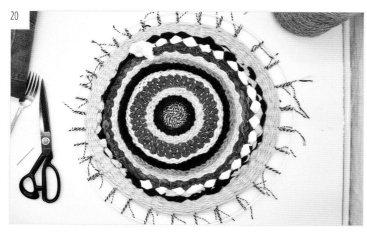

22. Before moving to the fringe, clean up any loose ends of weft at the back, and chop off all the warp strings (but not too short, since they can also be decorative).

23. Time to add the fringe. Loop the tassels around the last two weft rows all the way around the circle. I used the same yarn as at the very beginning (navy blue) and multiplied it to reach the necessary thickness. Cut any loops through and trim the edges of the fringe to tidy up.

The weaving is now ready. You can use it as is, or add a cushion to give a softer surface.

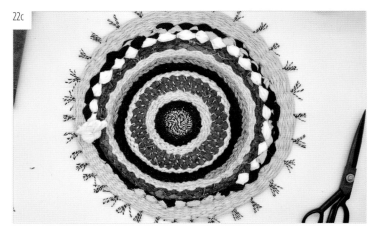

Three Circles Wall Hanging

This project makes an unusual wall hanging by using three circular frames as the motif. But this time after they are warped, they are woven as if they were on a frame loom.

For my frames I used the three inner rings of embroidery hoops, but you can use any suitable wooden or metallic frames or rings you can find. Whatever you choose, use three different complementary sizes.

All my measurements are based on using three rings of 7.8, 8.6, and 11 in. (20, 22, and 28 cm) diameter. Feel free to adjust the measurements according to your frames and to select your own yarns and colors. Here I am using recycled natural cotton string for the warp, and natural jute yarn (gardening twine) for the weft.

You will need:

3 circular frames, diameter 7.8, 8.6, and 11 in.

2 mm recycled cotton string (for the warp)

2 mm colored or natural yarn (gardening string)

Beater (fork)

Masking tape

Scissors

Tapestry needle

1. Begin by cutting pieces of string for the warp. To do this, place the two bigger frames one on the top of the other, so the bottom of the medium frame (8.6 in. diameter) touches the top of the large frame (11 in. diameter). Cut a piece of cotton string twice the dimension of the two diameters combined, plus 4 in. more on each end. Here, 2 x (8.6 + 11 + 4) = 48 in.

2. Cut an odd number of strings, depending on how wide you want your weaving area to be. (Here I cut fifteen pieces of cotton string to create a 3 in. wide weaving area.) Take one of the strings and loop it around the top of the medium frame (8.6 in. diameter), by going under the frame and inside into the loop.

3. Repeat the same with the rest of the strings.

Tip: I find it easiest to start with the middle warp string and then add one string at time on either side.

4. Put some tape on both sides of the top frame, close to the warp, to hold the frame in position.

5. Take the middle string and go straight to the bottom of the top medium frame and loop your string around it, by going over and around the frame. Now split the two ends to either side of the loop.

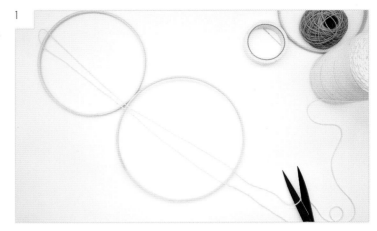

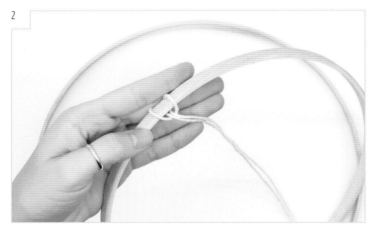

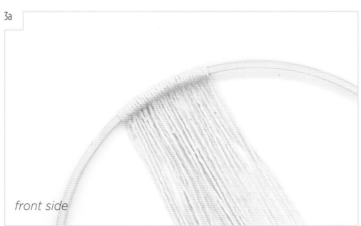

front side

3b

back side

4a

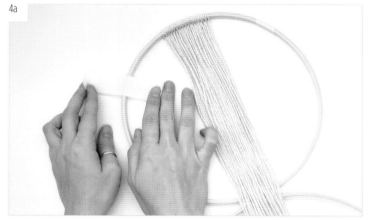

4b

5

6. Repeat the same process (step 5) on the large frame.

Go straight to the base of the large frame and loop the string again in the same way, but finish the ends together with a double knot. Make sure your string is straight, but not tight.

Tip: Leave your knot slightly loose, since you might need to readjust the tension of the warp later on.

7. Repeat the same with the rest of the warp strings. For an even tension, tie each string individually and alternately on each side of the central strand.

8. When you have finished all the tying, push the knots together with your fingers, so it is symmetrical with the very top of the warp.

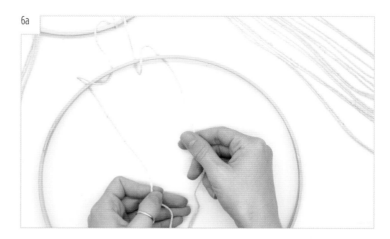

6a

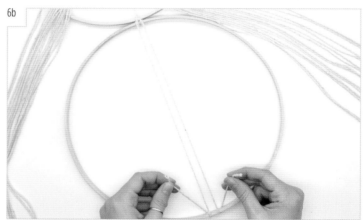

6b

6c

7a

7b

8a

8b

front side

8c

back side

9. Turn the two frames over so that you have the knots on the back side. On the large frame, thread your hand between pairs of warp strings—one pair up, next pair down—and insert the small frame into the space that you've created between the warp strings.

10. Push the small frame toward the top as far as it can go. Your warp setup is ready, and you can now start weaving.

11. Thread a long piece of weft yarn onto your tapestry needle. Using the two ends together, start weaving by going over two and under two warp ends.

12. Carry on weaving until you reach the top edge of the frame. Remember to beat down the weft from time to time as your design grows.

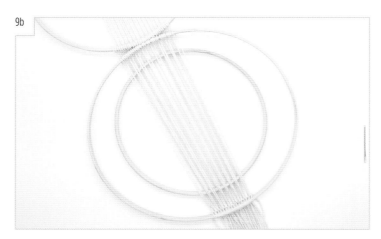

9b

10a

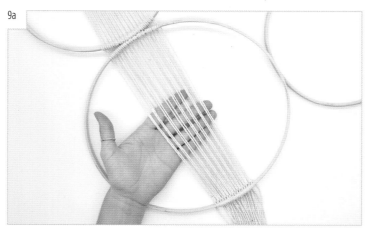

9a

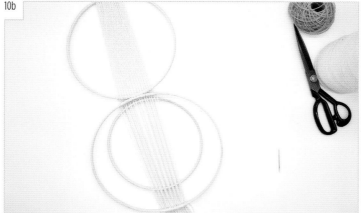

10b

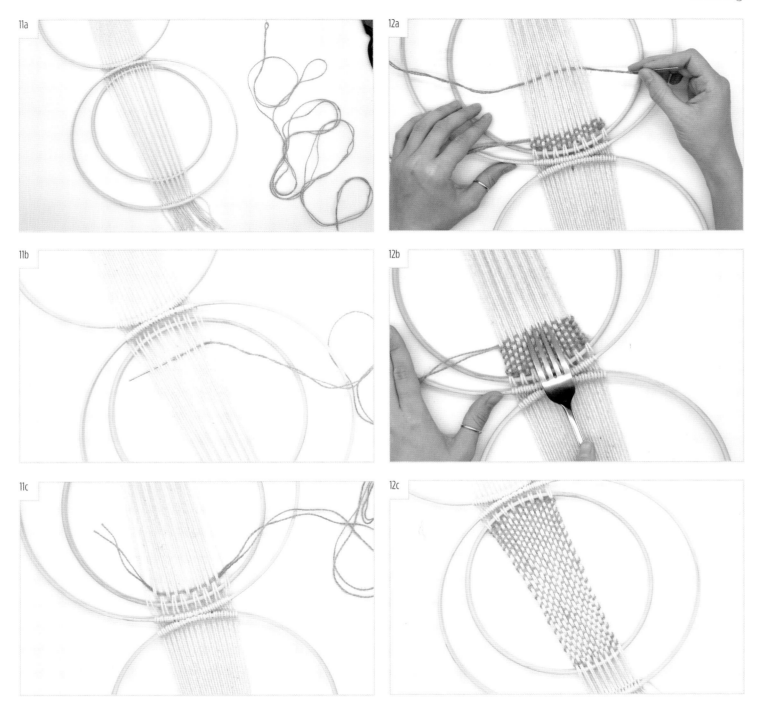

11a

11b

11c

12a

12b

12c

13. Continue weaving in exactly the same way onto the medium frame.

14. With your warp string, weave the small area at the base between the small and the large frames. Use a single yarn for the weft, but again go over and under two warp ends.

Note: If you haven't done this so far, check how tight your warp tension is, and readjust it as necessary by retying the knots at the bottom, before you return to weaving. You can check it by the roundness of the frames. If the large frame looks a bit oval, your tension is too tight and you need to make your warp looser—keep a close eye on the shape of your frame.

15. Now it's time to add short tassels around the small frame. Cut off pieces of wrap string (here about 3 in.) and, using two ends together, loop them under the frame and pull the ends through the loop (the same way you added tassels on a single warp in the "Frame Weaving" section).

16. Carry on until you have covered all the way around both sides of the small frame.

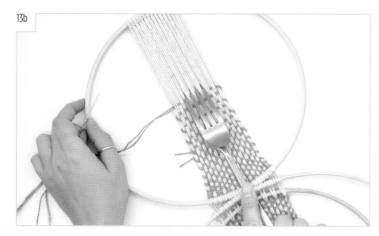

13b

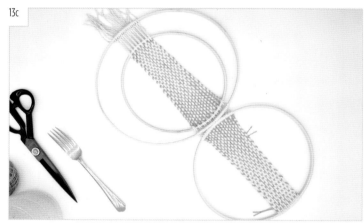

13c

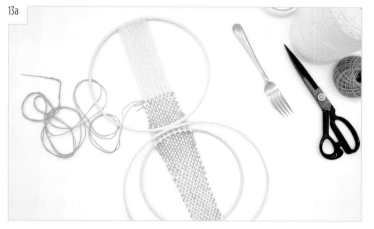

13a

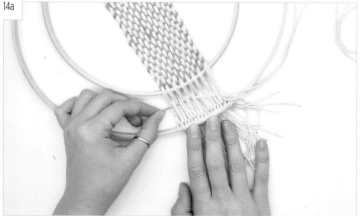

14a

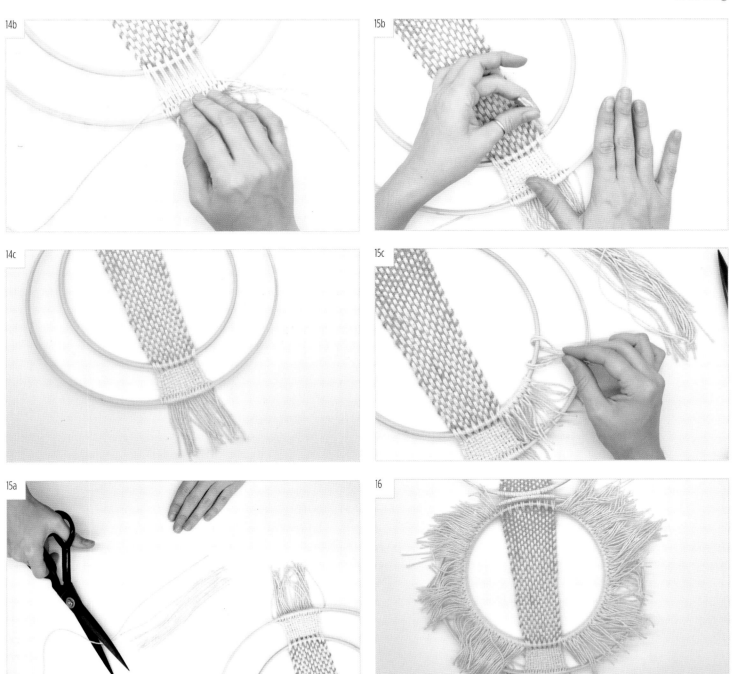

14b

14c

15a

15b

15c

16

17. Chop off the ends of your tassels to make them shorter and even.

18. With your tapestry needle (or a crochet hook, whichever you find easiest), bring the ends of the warp from the back side to the front side. Then chop them off to match the inner hoop fringe and make them nice and neat.

19. Now it's time to wrap your frames.
Turn your piece over onto the back and with your weft yarn tie a knot next to the warp at the base of the large frame, leaving a tail about 3 in. long. With a tapestry needle, secure this tail by going under a few warps.

20. Keeping a firm tension with your weft yarn, start wrapping the frame very tightly all the way around until you reach the top.

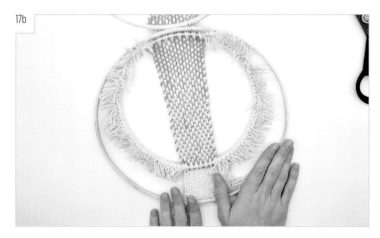

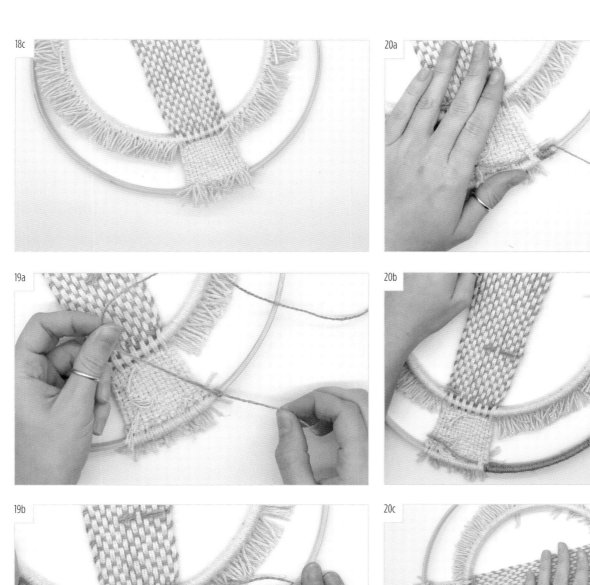

18c

19a

19b

20a

20b

20c

21. At the top, cut the yarn and, using the tapestry needle, go under one warp and then through the loop and pull it tight. Repeat that once. With your tapestry needle, secure the loose end of the wrapping yarn under a few warp ends.

22. Repeat the same on the other side of the frame.

23. With your warp string, repeat the same process on both sides of the top frame.

24. Cut some pieces of your weft yarn—about 6 in.—and add some tassels on top of the cotton string on both sides of the top frame.

Tip: Leave a bit of space in between the tassels to give a stripy effect to the frame.

23

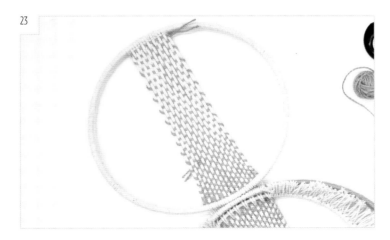

24a

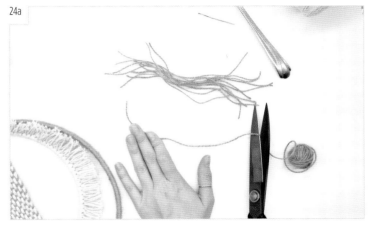

24b

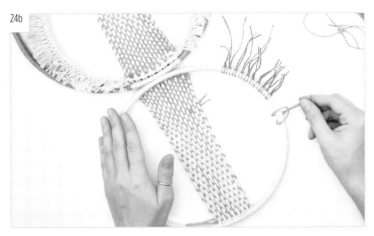

25. Trim the tassels to your preferred length.

26. Last, clean up any loose ends on the back.

Your new wall hanging is ready to go on your wall.

25b

25a

26

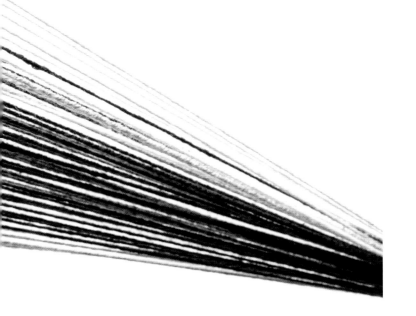

Band Weaving
on a Rigid
Heddle Board

Band Weaving on a Rigid Heddle Board

Band weaving—also called pickup weaving—is a technique for weaving narrow bands or ribbons that have both a high practical as well as aesthetic value. Such bands were produced by many cultures through history—they are variously called straps, backstraps, tapes, or belts—and were used for numerous purposes, such as for tying things, strapping, decorating, or simply holding textiles together. Their purposes, designs, and colors are endless.

The colors of these bands are usually chosen for contrast, while the patterns are created by the way the threads are picked up differently on each of the rows. This gives the maker the choice of limitless intricate patterns and the freedom to vary them at will.

Historically, band weaving comes from a time when having skillful hands was not only a necessity but also a highly valued attribute. Among other household activities, weaving cloth and spinning yarn for the needs of the household was the norm in almost all societies, regardless of geographical location.

Pickup bands were used for special occasions and as gifts that held symbolic value in celebrations such as weddings, christenings, coming-of-age ceremonies, and other important social occasions. Depending on the maker, the occasion, and the aesthetic characteristics of each area, these bands would vary in terms of complexity, color, and shape. Many examples held in museums are magnificent when it comes to their intricacy and aesthetic value.

As far as we know, the technique has remained pretty much the same since antiquity, meaning that we, too, can create wonderful things at home by using this centuries-old method of band weaving. The essential idea is very simple, and unlike conventional weaving, band weaving does not use a loom; instead the weaving is held in tension between the weaver's body and an anchor weight (for example, a door handle or heavy chair). Furthermore, the pattern is created by the warps—the long lengths of yarn—so it's these that need to be in color sequence. For this the weaver assembles a series of colored warps, then carefully threads them through a heddle board (also called a comb). The weft is, of course, still important but comprises a single color that is visible only at the edges. As the weft is worked from side to side, it reveals the woven design as it grows, but all the while the band is being firmly pulled, giving the maker control of the tightness.

The colored warps are threaded in sequence through the holes and slots on the heddle board. One end is held tightly by a belt on the weaver's waist, while the other end is attached to something solid, so the whole warp is held under tension by the weaver's body. The weaver lifts the heddle up and down, passes the shuttle (carrying the weft thread) between the warp threads, and tamps it down firmly with a beater.

The technique of band weaving can be used to create many different parts of textiles and clothing accessories, such as headbands, dress decoration, parts of men's clothing, straps and belts, ribbons, and handles. The heddle boards vary in size, shape, and material, but they are predominantly quite simple—just a comb-like board with combinations of long and narrow slots and holes for the warp to go through. You can find handmade as well as manufactured combs, constructed of anything from wood (the commonest) to modern materials such as plastic and acrylic.

Designing Your Piece

In band weaving, the warps are the threads that are most visible (compared to frame weaving), and the sequence of colors used on it determines the design of the woven piece. The weft is hidden in between the warp, and it is visible only at the sides. Remember this when designing your band.

With band weaving you can create very beautiful designs, as simple or complicated as you like. The final design of the band is determined by the sequence of the colors used on the warp, and the pattern on the band is determined by the sequence that the warp is threaded on the heddle board. There are plenty of patterns to follow (online and in weaving books), or you can create your own.

Band weaving requires careful planning of your piece, and it can get very complicated, but as an introduction I am going to keep it very simple. Decide what you are making, its pattern, how long you want it, and how wide. Choose your combination of warp yarns and a single complementary yarn for the weft. For your first attempt, the Decorative Band Belt with Tassels project, you'll use just four colors for the checkerboard pattern.

The woven band is created by lifting parts of the warp each time and inserting the weft. The warp will cover the weft, so what will be visible are rows consisting of warp yarns—this is your pattern. The most basic and commonest pattern is plain weave, which means that one row brings to the surface and makes visible all the odd warp yarns, and the next row brings to the surface and makes visible all the even warps. The back side will be the exact opposite—like positive and negative.

Things to keep in mind when planning your warp

Only half of the warp (evens or odds) will be visible. I find it helpful to think of it as two warps, where one sits on top of the other (giving two layers); see the Checkerboard pattern grid below. One layer is threaded through the evens slots, and the other through the odd slots. These change up and down with each pass of the shuttle.

Add a couple of ends on the sides of your warp of the same (or very similar) color as your weft (see belt sample image below). That way you will create a border at the edges that blends nicely with the weft loops.

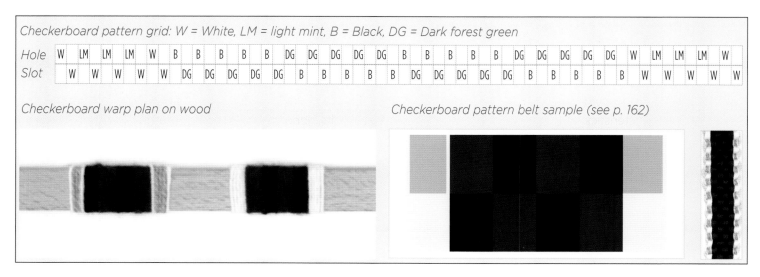

Checkerboard pattern grid: W = White, LM = light mint, B = Black, DG = Dark forest green

Hole	W	LM	LM	LM	W	B	B	B	B	B	DG	DG	DG	DG	DG	B	B	B	B	B	DG	DG	DG	DG	DG	W	LM	LM	LM	W
Slot		W	W	W	W	W	DG	DG	DG	DG	DG	B	B	B	B	B	B	DG	DG	DG	DG	DG	B	B	B	B	B	W	W	W	W	W

Checkerboard warp plan on wood

Checkerboard pattern belt sample (see p. 162)

Width of the Warp

A good practical way to plan your warp is to try out and test your yarns and colors. Do this by wrapping your chosen yarns around a piece of cardboard or wood, so you can see exactly how the colors look next to each other. Play around with their stripes and thicknesses. Also, it's important to actually count the number of ends your piece will have—this will determine the final width of your woven band.

Remember, each yarn will go through one of the slots or holes of the heddle board. So you need to have a total maximum number of warp ends no greater than your heddle board's number of slots and holes.

Note: I make two wraps for each warp: one for the long slots of the heddle board and one for the small holes.

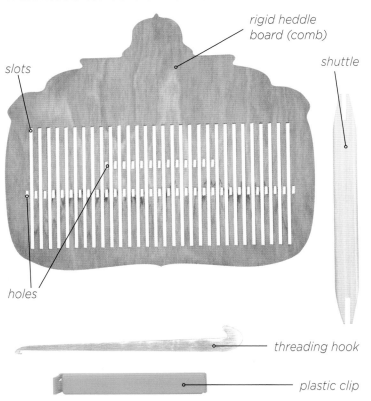

slots

holes

rigid heddle board (comb)

shuttle

threading hook

plastic clip

Length of the Warp

The length of your warp depends on what you want to weave, since you are not constrained by the size of your heddle board. However, remember that you will need proportionately more thread/yarn than the length of your final piece.

You will need about 20 inches more than the final length for each warp, since the yarns will go up and down and be filled with the weft, plus you will also need a bit extra for tying up. In addition, the last 14 inches are not weaveable, since the loom will be very close to the tying point.

Warp Thread Characteristics

Your choice of warp yarns should be carefully considered, since these will form the foundation of your fabric and will determine the design of your woven piece. The thread should be strong and smooth and able to withstand the friction and stretching of weaving. Additionally, if you use more than one color, it is important that all your warp yarns have the same thickness; otherwise your band will be uneven and the pattern will likely be distorted. The yarns must also be able to go comfortably through the slots in the loom.

You can use any weaving or knitting yarn, cotton string, thread, or twine that has a thickness of about a four-ply fingering yarn (4/18 NM, sock weight). More-advanced weavers work with yarns measured in epi or wpi—ends or wraps per inch (both mean the same measurement). So 12 epi (or wpi) means twelve ends (or wraps) per inch—measured by wrapping your yarn around a ruler and counting how many ends fit in an inch. But such refinements need not bother us at this early stage.

Example of 12 epi and 14 epi yarns.

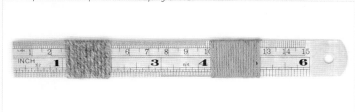

Tip: *If you have a very thin yarn, you can use two or three ends for each warp yarn and thread them through the same slot. However, I suggest you don't complicate matters like this for your first attempt at band weaving.*

Warp Suggestions
- alpaca
- bamboo
- cotton
- linen
- wool

The Process

1. Design the warp: Decide on pattern, colors, width, and length. To work this out, make two yarn wraps, one for each layer of warp (evens/odds—slots/holes).

2. Warping: Cut the number of ends (i.e., the number of lengths of yarn) each warp layer needs (remembering to add the extra needed for tying up and so on) to the desired length by using a warping mill/frame or a large picture frame.

3. Threading: Thread (pull) the warp through the slots and holes on the loom, using a threading hook.

4. Tie one end of the warp onto something solid (door handle / clamp on table) and grab the other end with a plastic clip, and with a string or bathrobe belt, attach the clip to your waist. Make sure the warp is tight and that all the ends have the same tension across the width.

5. Weave: By lifting the heddle board, the warp will be separated into evens and odds (or top and bottom layers). Pass the shuttle across the weft through the shed (warp opening) and pull tight.

6. By pulling the loom down, the warp will be separated into evens and odds. Pass the shuttle across the weft and through the shed and pull tight.

7. Repeat steps 5 and 6 until you have woven your desired length of band. Every few inches, release the clip around your waist, pull the woven strip toward you, then reattach it closer, so the weaving area is always near you.

Note: *Since the yarns are close to each other, they might be a bit sticky, so each time you will need to separate the two layers with your fingers before you insert the shuttle.*

Making the Warp

In order to warp your heddle board, you first need to make your warp. Cut out the number of ends (lengths of yarn) your warp needs to the desired length, not forgetting to include the necessary extra length.

The best way to do this is to have all the ends in tension—stretch them by tying them on something solid that won't move. There's special equipment for this—a warping frame or warping mill—but you can instead either tie one end to something rigid, such as a door handle or table clamp, and stretch out the full length by walking back and forth to order the warp. Or use a large picture frame, a table, or a couple of heavy chairs and warp the yarns around it.

To demonstrate the warping technique, I have used a picture frame. This way you can get the lengths of the warp without walking up and down numerous times between one end and the other.

Warping

You will need:
Rigid heddle board (comb)
Large picture frame (or warping frame/mill)
3 colored yarns (14 epi)
Cotton twine
Measuring tape
Scissors
Threading hook (or a small-numbered crochet hook)

1. After designing your warp and deciding its width, length, and number of ends, take your cotton string and cut out the length you need plus 20 in. Use this first string as your guide to cut the rest of your yarn lengths. I have decided that my final piece will be about 32–35 in., so I cut the cotton string to that length, plus 20 in. extra, plus a bit more for tying up the string on the frame. This setup needs to be done in color order to make threading the heddle straightforward.

Warp setup:
Long slots: 2 white—9 purple—2 white
Small holes: 2 white—9 gray—2 white

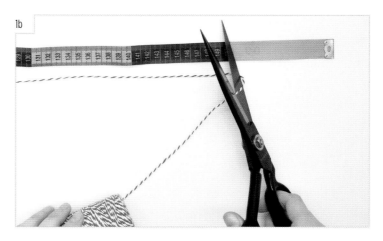

2. To get your warps in color order for threading on the heddle board, tie one end of your string on the bottom left of the frame.

3. Warp the string around the frame, then tie up the other end. Look at the photo: create a route for the warp yarns to follow, using the maximum possible length of the string.

Note: If your string cannot reach a side of the frame to tie it up, just add a bit more string. It is better to have a longer warp than shorter.

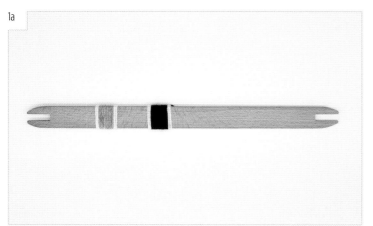

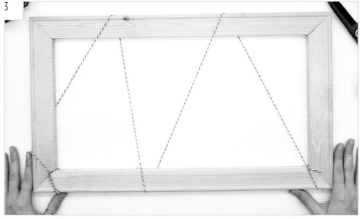

4. Then, by following your warp setup, tie up the first warp yarn and follow the yarn guide back and forth across the picture frame for as many times as your warps need. I have started with the white thread and will warp it twice.

5. Carry on with your next color: here, nine times with gray yarn. It is advisable not to tie the yarn end onto the frame, but to tie it to the next yarn and carry on. You might not be able to avoid ending your warp on this side, but do it as little as possible.

Note: If you have an odd number of warp ends, you will finish wrapping at the other end.

6. Continue with the next color—here, the last two white ends—and cut off the yarn. If you have finished at the end of the cotton guide, tie your yarn on the previous knot of gray and white yarn. If you have finished at the beginning of the guide, just tie your yarn on the frame as normal.

7. Cut off the loop at the starting point of your warp.

8. Place a string at the other end of your warp. Make a loop with the string, put it under the yarns, and pull the two ends of the string through the loop. Make sure you have a long piece of string, since you will use it to tie your warp onto something solid to hold it in place.

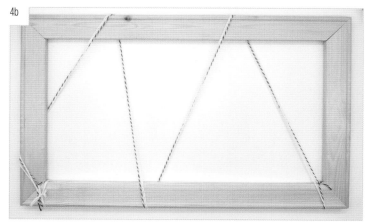

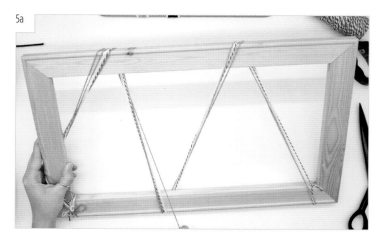

5b

7

6a

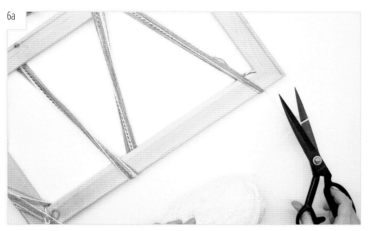

8a

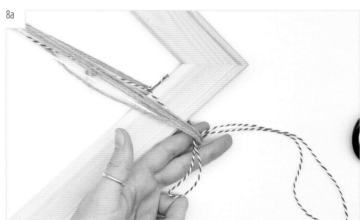

6b

8b

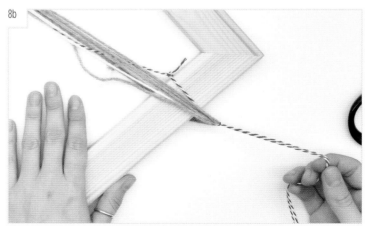

9. Pull your warp out of the frame and wind it into a ball. The first half of your warp is ready.

10. Repeat the same process with the other half of the warp, this time in preparation for the long slots. Remember to use your cotton string to create your warp path.

You are now ready to start threading your loom.

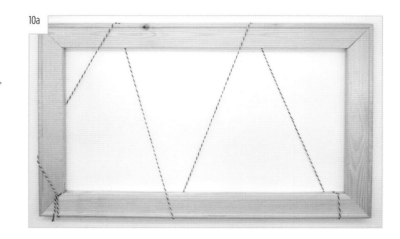

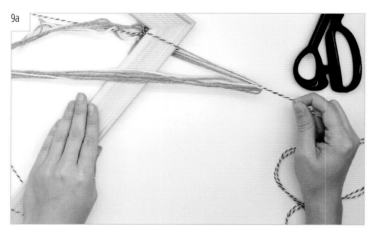

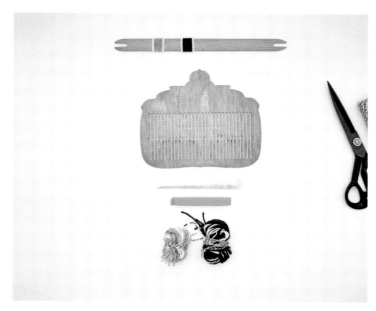

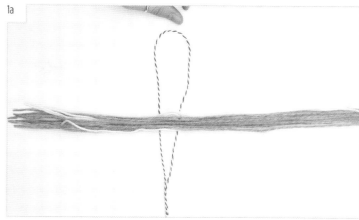

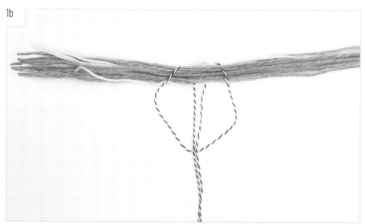

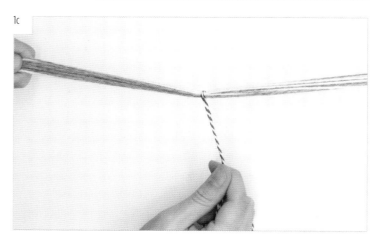

Threading

You will need:
Rigid heddle (comb) board
Cotton string
Clip
Threading hook

1. Tie the end of the warp somewhere rigid: for example, to a door, window handle, or clamp on a table. (See step 8 on p. 148, where you created a loop to attach your warp.) Then cut a long string, place the middle of it under the cut end of your warp, and pull the top ends of the ring through the loop and tighten.

Note: I am using only the central slots and holes of my heddle board because I am making only a narrow band.

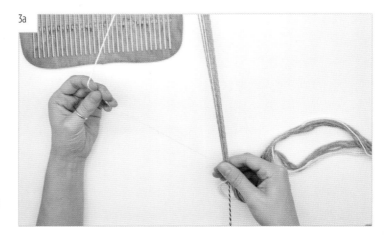

2. Tie the string around your waist (by using more string or a belt, so the whole warp is stretched). Having your warp under tension will make the threading much easier.

3. By following your warp setup, extract the first yarn from your tied-off warp ends, and with the threading hook pull it from the back through the first small hole. Here I am threading the white end through the top series of small holes.

4. Carry on with the rest of ends, following your warp setup.

5. When you have threaded a few warp ends, it makes the job easier if you keep the threaded ends under tension as well. To do so, cut a long piece of string, place the middle of it into a clip, and tie it to your wrist or the table (using a clamp). Then catch the threaded warp ends with the clip to stretch them.

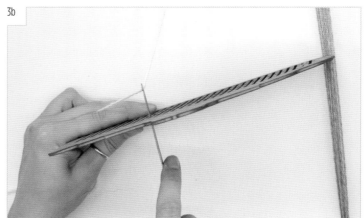

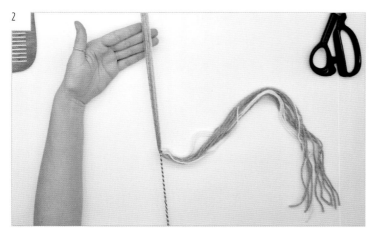

4a

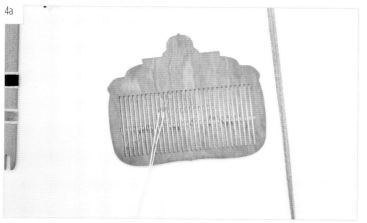

5a

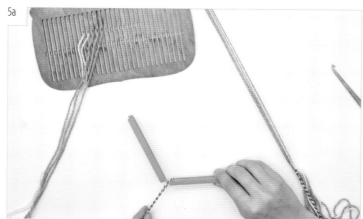

4b

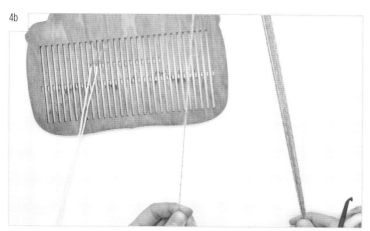

5b

4c

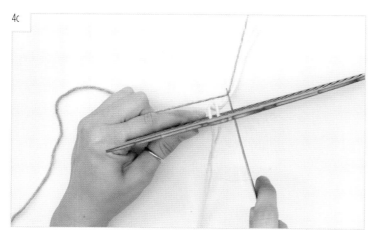

6. Carry on until you have threaded all the ends of the first half of the warp.

7. Repeat the same process with the other half of your warp, this time threading it through the long slots on the rigid heddle board (comb).

8. Combine the ends of the two parts of the warp. Hold the end firmly and, with the fingers of your other hand, go through the warp a few times, as if brushing it. This evens up the wrap ends, thus giving all the warp ends the same tension. It is really very important to have the same tension across the whole warp while weaving.

9. When you have achieved a good tension, catch your warp with the clip (which is tied to your waist or the table) and you are ready to weave.

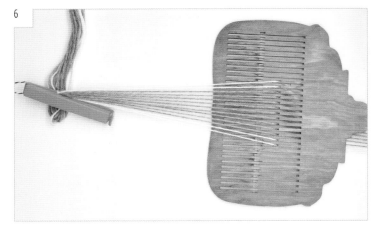

6

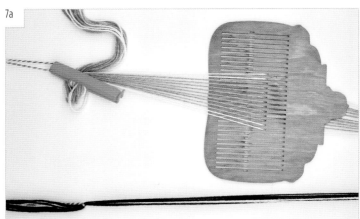

7a

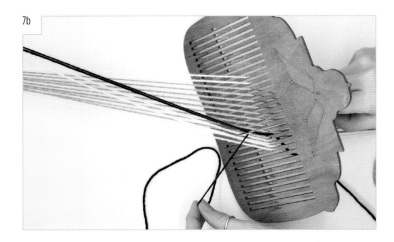

7b

7c
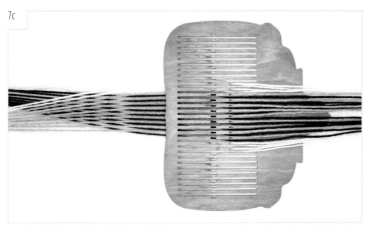

9a
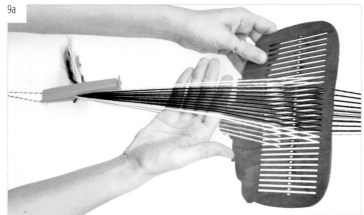

8a
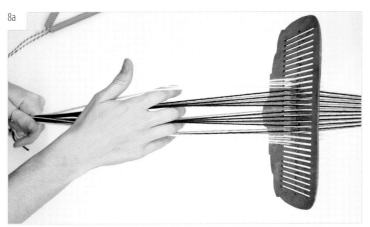

9b
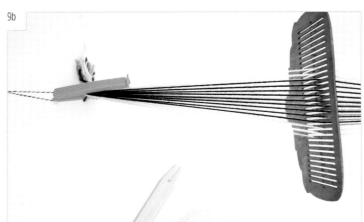

8b

3. Carry on by repeating steps 1 and 2.

The importance of tension

You need to pull your weft tightly—not too tight, but definitely not loose. Try a few rows with different tension until you get it right. Remember that your final band will have the width of your wrapping, even if the ends are spread out on the heddle board.

If you can't get a good tension on the weft and the band looks wobbly, recheck the tension of the warp. To do so, tie the beginning of your warp somewhere solid, then go to the other end and stretch it and "brush" it with your fingers a few times. If it needs a lot of adjustment, you might need to cut the end loop and retie the string and the whole warp.

Correct tension is the key to successful weaving.

Weaving

You will need your weft yarn, a shuttle, and scissors.

If this is your first time weaving with a heddle board, I suggest you try a few different thicknesses for the weft to see which one you like the most, then keep this sample warp as a reference.

I used three different yarns:
Chunky white wool
Fine white knitting bamboo yarn (sock weight)
Medium-thickness bleached linen

1. First, wind your yarn on the shuttle (I started with linen). Then pull your heddle board down so you separate the warp and create a shed for the shuttle to go through. Pass the shuttle with your weft through the shed and push the yarn down (use your finger or a fork).

2. Pull the heddle board up so the other half of the warp comes up to the top. Put your finger into the shed and push the warp toward the previous weft row. Then insert your shuttle through the shed and pull it gently to loop around the side.

4. Continue weaving. If you are trying different thicknesses on the weft, you can cut off the first one and insert the second one. Leave the loose ends hanging out so you know where each yarn is woven. Here I have moved to the thinner, bamboo knitting yarn, and you can see that the rows have become a bit thinner and the width of the band gets a bit narrower as well.

5. When you have woven your desired length, just cut off the weft but leave a long tail for the finishing. If you want tassels at the end, leave a tail a bit longer than you want them to be.

Note: I wove the last section with rug wool. You can see that the rows are much thicker and the band a bit wider.

1

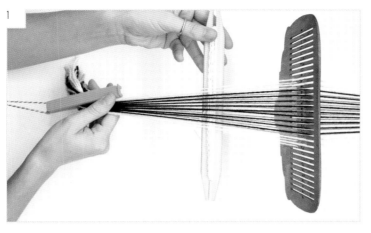

2

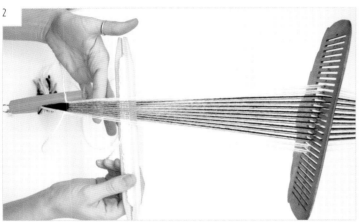

3a

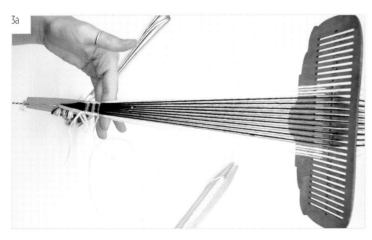

3b

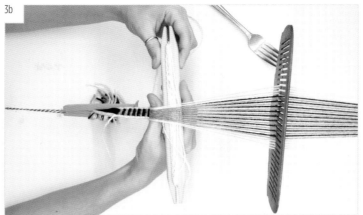

4

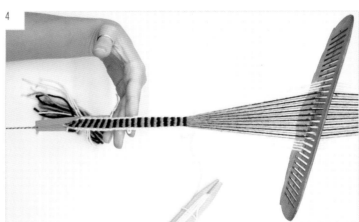

5

Finishing

Cutting Off the Heddle Board

1. To remove your piece from the heddle board, you need to untie the end of the warp from your anchor (the door handle or clamp). Cut off the end loop of the warps.

2. Last, just pull the rest of the warp off the heddle board. You can see here the clear differences of thickness produced by the different wefts.

Finishing the Weave

1. First secure the weft at the beginning and the end of the band. For this, just make a double knot with the weft and one of the side ends of the warp of the same or similar color very close to the edge. It will then be hidden from the rest of the warp. You should also cut off any loose ends of weft along the length of the band. However, since this is a sample band, you can skip that part.

You now have two options: braid ends, or tassels with a bead.

Option 1: Braid ends

2. Tie one end of the band up somewhere solid and braid the loose ends of the warp at the other end.

3. Catch the end of the braid with your clip. Pick a piece of yarn (one of the yarns on the warp) and wrap it around the end of the braid, then tie it up to secure the braid. To do that, loop your yarn and place it under the braid and then pull the ends of the yarn through the loop.

4. Then split the two ends and wrap them around (clockwise and counterclockwise accordingly) and after a few rounds make a double knot with them.

5. Last, chop off the warp ends to your desired length.

Option 2: Tassels with a bead

6. Thread the warp ends though the bead. Use a tapestry needle if it helps.

7. Secure the loose ends as before in steps 3 and 4 of option 1.

8. Chop off the ends to the length you want.

Note: You could combine the options above or you could also leave the ends free and use the warp as tassels. Experiment with different finishing techniques and find the one that you like best for your band.

Last, it is advisable (but optional) to gently wash your band after weaving it, in order to get rid of any oily residue or coating that may have come from the industrial spinning/handling process of the yarns. Washing the yarns will hydrate them and make them fluffier and softer.

Wash your handwoven band very gently. This is particularly important with any piece that contains wool: friction, heat, and water can make the fabric felt, which of course could be part of your plan, but be aware of it. However, I do suggest that you not be afraid of washing your band and that you experiment with different temperatures and methods of washing—handwash or washing machine and tumble dryer.

General washing instructions:
• Handwash your band in a maximum of 86°F water with a gentle detergent—either a nonbiological or one made especially for wool and delicates.
• Rinse the band several times to make sure all the detergent has been removed. The water should be clear when you finish.
• Gently squeeze the water out of your band—you can take any excess water off by using a towel.
• Let it dry—flat if possible.

Your sample band is ready.

3a

3b

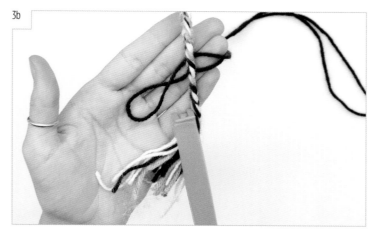

3c

4

5

6

7

8

Decorative Band Belt with Tassels

These step-by-step instructions make a beautiful belt about 60 inches long, with a design inspired by a classic check. Feel free to amend the dimensions as you want and your loom allows, and make sure to choose your favorite colors.

You will need:
Rigid heddle board (comb)
4 colored yarns for the warp (T-shirt yarn)
Cotton string
4 bamboo knitting yarns (12 epi)—white, light mint, black, dark forest green
Bathrobe belt or similar (optional)
Clip
Measuring tape
Scissors
Shuttle
Threading hook
Natural white cotton T-shirt yarn for the weft

Warp setup:
Part 1: 1 white, 3 light mint, 1 white, 5 black, 5 dark forest green, 5 black, 5 dark forest green, 1 white, 3 light mint, 1 white
Part 2: 5 white, 5 dark forest green, 5 black, 5 dark forest green, 5 black, 5 white

Length: 8 ft. (2.44 m)—for a 60 in. (1.52 m) long belt, plus tassels

1. Make your warp on a frame (or warping mill/frame) as described on p. 146.

2. Thread both sets of warp, one through the long slots (**2a-b**), and the other through the central smaller holes (**2c-d**).

3. Tie the two ends of the warp together and adjust the tension (**3a**). Remember you need to have a very tight, even tension right across the entire warp (**3b**). Tie up the start of the warp with a string around your waist (or on a belt).

4. Weave a few rows of your weft, using the same white yarn as you used for the warp. Remember to keep it tight. This step is optional, and you can instead start weaving straight away with the T-shirt yarn. However, I find that weaving the beginning with a thin yarn helps even up the tension, and furthermore I like having a thinner beginning (and ending) to my belt.

5. After a few rows, start weaving the weft with the T-shirt yarn. In order to change yarns (or if you have run out and you need to add some more), insert the new yarn in the last row of the previous yarn, so you have two wefts in one row. This action also secures the weft so it is easy to cut the loose ends off afterward without the risk of them unraveling. Additionally, to secure the edges of the band, you need to insert it from the opposite direction of the previous yarn. This means you will end up with a loose end on both sides of the band. Last, make sure the tail hanging off the new (T-shirt) yarn is long enough to weave one row.

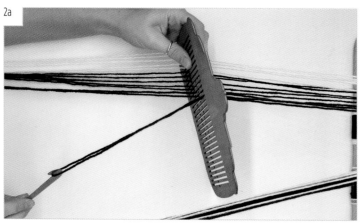

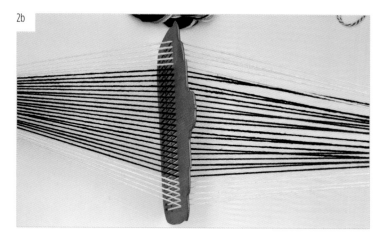

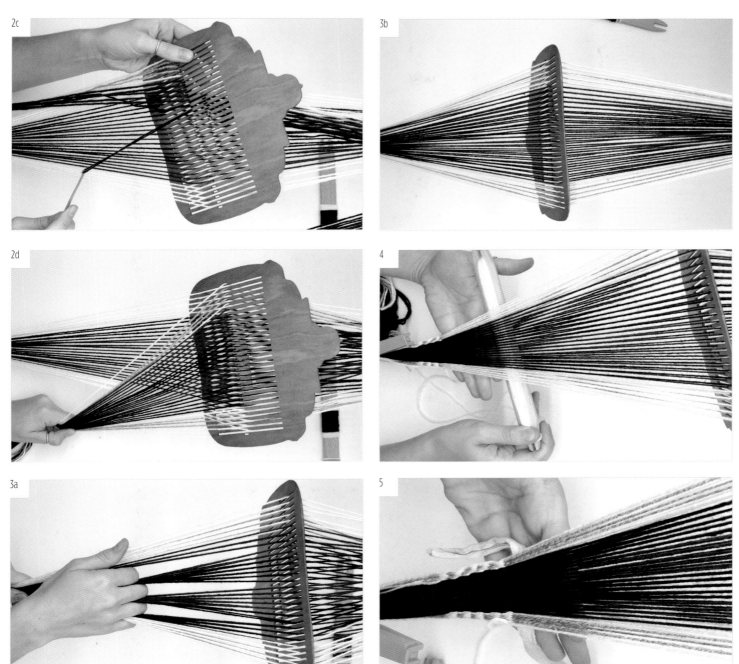

2c

2d

3a

3b

4

5

6. On the next row, for extra safety, also weave in the loose end of the new (T-shirt) yarn. Continue weaving until you have woven the length you need.

7. Cut the woven piece off the loom and secure your weft at both ends.

8. Cut off any loose weft ends.

9. Chop the warp ends to make tassels as long as you like—then trim them.

And your new belt is ready. Enjoy!

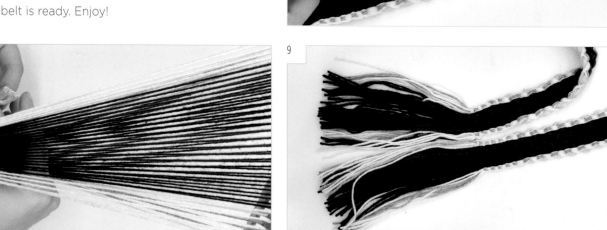

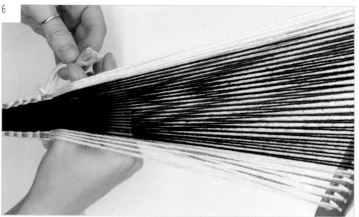

Bag Strap with Long Tassels

This project shows you how to make an elegant handmade strap for your tote bag or, indeed, any other bag you want. You can either make it long enough for a cross-body bag or cut it into two pieces and instead use them as handles. Change the dimensions according to your body and your bag—also pick your favorite colors to coordinate with your favorite bag.

You will need:
Rigid heddle board (comb)
Bathrobe belt or similar (optional)
Black cotton knitting yarn—for the weft
Clip
4 colored cotton knitting yarn (14 epi)—white, black, navy blue, coral pink—for the warp
Measuring tape
Scissors
Shuttle
Striped cotton string
Threading hook
Tote bag

Warp setup:
Part 1 (23 ends): 2 black, 8 coral pink, 3 white, 8 navy blue, 2 black
Part 2 (22 ends): 2 black, 8 navy blue, 2 white, 8 coral pink, 2 black
Length: 8 ft. (2.44 m): for a 55 in. (1.40 m) strap, plus approximately 12 in. (30.5 cm) tassels for each side)

1. Make your warp on a large frame (or a warping mill/frame) as described in the "Band Weaving on a Rigid Heddle Board: Warping" section on pp. 146-150). Make sure that you keep the same tension while wrapping your yarns.

2. Thread both parts one by one, with your threading hook.

Thread the first group through the long slots (**2a–b**) and the other group through the smaller holes (**2c–d**). If your loom has more slots than the number of warp ends, make sure that you center your warp and that you leave the same number of slots empty on both sides.

3. Tie the two ends of the warp together and, using your fingers, comb through the warp threads to adjust the tension. Remember this tension needs to be very tight and the same across all the warp.

4. Tie up the beginning of the warp with a string (or onto a belt) around your waist and start weaving with your weft yarn. (Since my black yarn is quite thin and I want my strap to be quite thick, I have doubled up the ends of weft on the shuttle.)

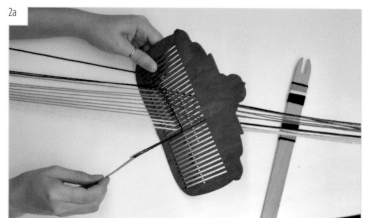

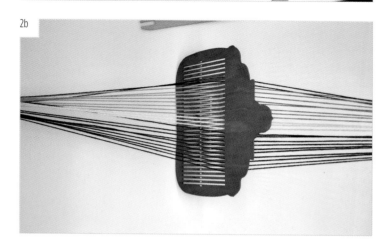

2c
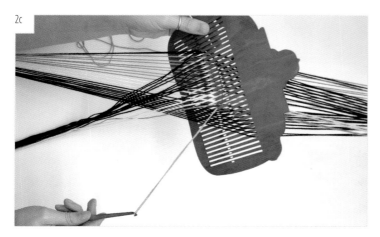

3b

2d
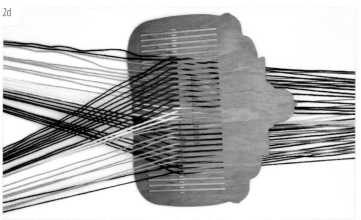

4
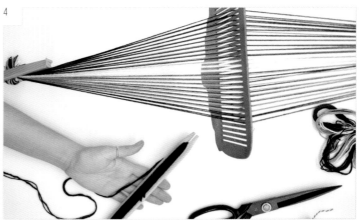

3a
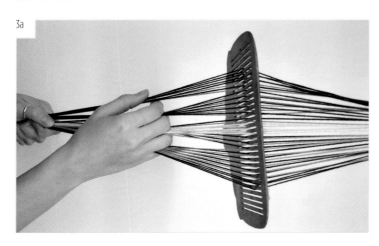

5. Weave one row with your weft and leave a long tail, about an inch longer than the width of your strap.

6. On the next row, weave the weft tail in with your fingers and then weave in your weft with the shuttle.

7. Pull both ends until you get the correct band width.

8. Carry on weaving. If something doesn't look right or feel nice, check your tension on both the weft and warp.

9. When you have woven your chosen length (55 in.), cut your piece off the board.

10. Secure the weft by tying it in with one of the warp ends of the same color.

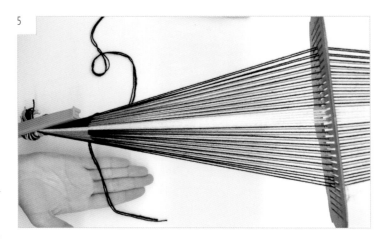

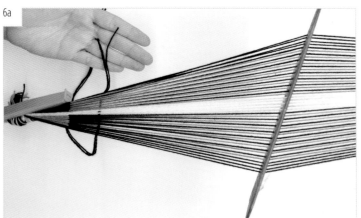

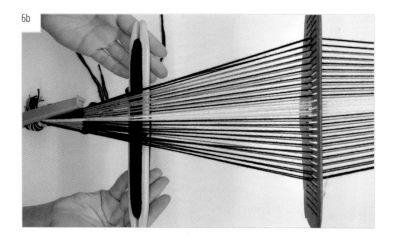

7

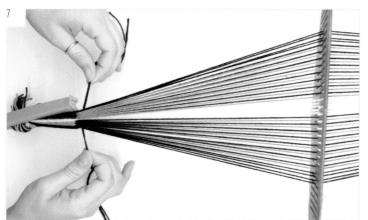

8c

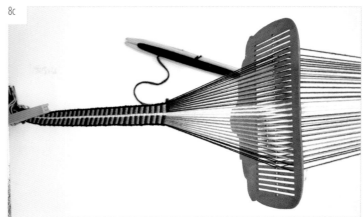

8a

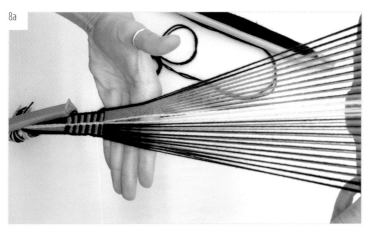

9

8b

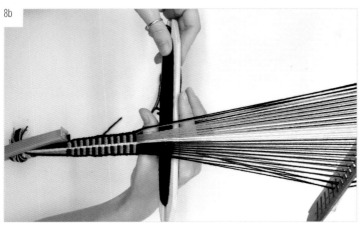

10

11. Cut off any loose ends of weft. Last, stitch your band onto your bag to the length you need, according to your height, and you're ready.

Enjoy your new bag!

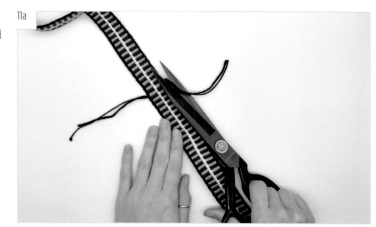
11a

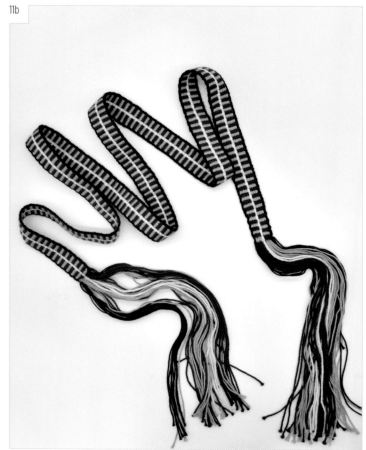
11b

About the Author

Maria is a professional textile designer, weaver, and teacher. Under her brand name Maria Sigma | Woven Textiles, she produces contemporary zero waste textiles for interiors for residential and commercial spaces from her studio in London. Maria teaches monthly "Weaving From Waste" workshops around the UK and in her native Greece.

After studies in textile conservation in Greece, Maria went on to complete a degree in textile design at Chelsea College of Art and Design in London. She has twice been the recipient of the Cockpit Arts/"Clothworkers" Award, in 2015 and 2016. In 2017 she received investment support from The Prince's Trust and Virgin Start-Up Scheme. With their support she invested in a new loom and a studio space in London.

Maria handweaves her fabrics on a wooden floor loom in a process that has hardly changed for centuries. Her dedication to a zero-waste philosophy and her sustainable work ethic can be seen throughout the design and manufacture process. She eschews dyes as they require large amounts of water and her careful weaving and cutting technique minimizes yarn waste. Her handwoven, undyed textile collection has a raw simplicity that appeals to the 21st century search for honest, ethical, and nurturing materials for the home.

Maria's commitment to sustainable living has led her to start workshops teaching others how to weave from waste fabrics and old clothes. She also sells starter weaving kits with bespoke color palettes which are the perfect addition to this book so readers can try this ancient and meditative craft at home. *www.mariasigma.com*

Her work has been featured in *House & Gardens*, *The Observer*, *Sunday Times*, *Elle Decoration*, *The Country Living*, *The Telegraph*, *Monocle*, *Hole & Corner*, *Reclaim Magazine* and more. She has collaborated internationally with renowned interior studios and brands including Soho House, TOAST, and J.M.S Furniture.

Acknowledgments and Resources

The completion of this book could not have been possible without the participation and assistance of so many people who actively assisted me over the course of working on it. Not forgetting my workshop students, to whom this whole series is also inspired by and based on.

To Jo Bryant, whose encouraging guidance and patience has helped immensely.

Zondag, Elena, Anastasios, and Alex for their endless support, kindness, and understanding spirit during the writing of this book.

Special thanks to Alex for the technical support and to Zondag for giving me all her waste T-shirts and old jeans.

To all my relatives, friends, and others who in one way or another shared their support morally and physically—a heartfelt thank-you.

- A Verb for Keeping Warm (USA)
  www.averbforkeepingwarm.com
- Ashford Wheels & Looms (New Zealand)
  www.ashford.co.nz
- Camilla Valley Farm Weavers' Supply (Canada)
  http://camillavalleyfarm.com
- Cattywampus Crafts (USA)
  www.cattywampuscrafts.com
- Fibre Maven (Canada)
  www.fibremaven.com
- Frank Herring & Sons Ltd. (UK)
  www.frankherringandsons.com
- George Weil & Sons Ltd. (UK)
  www.georgeweil.com
- Glimåkra (Sweden)
  www.gavglimakra.se/en
- Habu Textiles (Japan)
  www.habutextiles.com
- Laine-et-tricot (France)
  www.en.laine-et-tricot.com
- Loop (UK)
  www.loopknittingshop.com
- Stoorstålka (Sweden)
  https://shop.stoorstalka.com/en/start.html
- The Handweavers Studio & Gallery (UK)
  http://handweavers.co.uk
- The Threshing Barn (UK)
  https://threshingbarn.com
- Tribe Yarn (UK)
  www.tribeyarns.com
- Vävstuga Weaving School (USA)
  www.vavstuga.com
- Weaver House Co. (USA)
  www.weaverhouseco.com
- Weft Blown (UK)
  www.weftblown.com
- Wool Inspires (Luxembourg)
  http://woolinspires.com/fr